A History of College Church in Wheaton

A History of
COLLEGE CHURCH
in Wheaton

• The First 150 Years •

EDITH L. BLUMHOFER

Tyndale House Publishers, Inc.
Carol Stream, Illinois

For Wendell Hawley, with appreciation and esteem

Visit Tyndale's exciting Web site at www.tyndale.com.

TYNDALE and Tyndale's quill logo are registered trademarks of Tyndale House Publishers, Inc.

A History of College Church in Wheaton: The First 150 Years

Designed by Timothy R. Botts

Edited by Bonne L. Steffen

Scripture quotations are taken from the *Holy Bible*, King James Version.

ISBN 978-1-4143-4832-2
Printed in the United States of America

16 15 14 13 12 11 10
7   6   5   4   3   2   1

CONTENTS

CHAPTER 1
BEGINNINGS

Hear'st thou, O God! those chains,
That clank on Freedom's plains,
By Christians wrought?
Those who these chains have worn,
Christians from home have torn,
Christians have hither borne,
Christians have bought!

JOHN PIERPONT, in *A Collection of Psalms and Hymns for the*
Wesleyan Methodist Connection of America, 1845

THE BEGINNINGS OF COLLEGE CHURCH IN WHEATON reach back to the mid-nineteenth-century heyday of American evangelicalism and Protestant hopes for a Christian America. The congregation's story is a microcosm of the larger Protestant story of hopes and disappointments, cooperation and contention, growth and reconfiguration. The social activism of the Wesleyan Methodist Connection with its anti-slavery crusading spirit, the missionary zeal of Illinois Congregationalists with their exhilarating vision for education and evangelism, and the strong personality of Jonathan Blanchard, who brought New England sensibilities to the frontier, combined to shape an evangelical congregation characterized by social concern, revivalist sympathies, and a commitment to education. College Church, Wheaton College, and the community of Wheaton grew up together, and each indelibly marked the others.

The story actually begins before the town of Wheaton was

platted in 1853. Settlers began trickling into Milton Township at about the same time that the Black Hawk War (1832) pushed Native Americans across the Mississippi River. Among them were several families of Chadwicks who came by Conestoga wagon from upstate New York and New England. Hardy men and women of Protestant faith, the Chadwicks and other early settlers of DuPage County brought to Illinois their strong opinions on the issues that agitated in the older states–states' rights, territorial expansion, the Bank of the United States, slavery.

In the winter of 1843, Joseph and Alvira Chadwick met a "fire-eating anti-slavery man" named Rufus Lumry. A Methodist circuit rider in Illinois since the 1830s, Lumry quarreled with his superiors who refused to denounce slavery. A group of Methodists had recently seceded from their denomination to take a clearer stand against slavery and for representative church government. When this group proposed to make Lumry their representative in northern Illinois, he promptly agreed. He exploited his connections in the interests of anti-slavery Methodism. Lumry easily persuaded the Chadwicks and their neighbors to form a congregation of the new Wesleyan Methodist Connection. In February 1843, fourteen people met in the Chadwick home to do so. The Wesleyan Connection was the first church to be organized in the area that later became known as Wheaton. The infant denomination's weekly publication, *The True Wesleyan*, linked these members in far-off Illinois to like-minded people across the Northeast.

A direct line leads from that house meeting (near what is now the Chicago Golf Club in Wheaton) to Wheaton College, the First Church of Christ in Wheaton, and College Church. First Presbyterian Church in Wheaton and Wheaton Bible Church share the lineage too. Particular perspectives on the larger religious and cultural questions of the times directly shaped the beginnings of these Wheaton congregations, influenced their networking, and inspired their community activism.

The Wesleyan Methodist Connection

Wesleyan Methodists saw themselves as the true descendants of the sixty itinerant Methodist circuit-riding preachers who met in Baltimore in 1784 to organize the Methodist Episcopal Church and evangelize the new United States. Under the direction of John Wesley's handpicked superintendent, Francis Asbury, these men embraced the ambitious goal of evangelizing the rapidly expanding nation. Asbury set the example, preaching daily wherever people gathered, and averaging 6,000 miles on horseback each year. When he died in 1816, American Methodists numbered 700 preachers and more than 214,000 members. Though Methodist ranks included some prosperous farmers with middle-class pretensions, for the most part ordinary men and women filled Methodist pews. Regular revivals and camp meetings kept enthusiasm high, weekly lay-led class meetings promoted accountability, and circuit riders carried the democratic Methodist message to the remotest parts of the frontier:

Come, sinner, to the gospel feast!
Let every soul be Jesus' guest;
You need not one be left behind,
For God has bidden all mankind.

The pace of Methodist growth caused some insiders to worry that enthusiasm for evangelism obscured John Wesley's "peculiar doctrine" of Christian perfection. To safeguard this "grand depositum of Methodism," they formed the holiness movement to promote Wesley's heartfelt call to inward purity. Their concern for spiritual perfection soon overflowed into movements for social reform: Wesley's "social holiness" focused first on the spiritual state of the believing community, but the pursuit of godliness brought awareness of public as well as private evils, one of which was slavery.

The issue of slavery

In the 1820s, growing numbers of Methodists watched in dismay as their thriving denomination gradually abandoned its historic stance against slavery. By the late 1830s, Methodist preachers with abolitionist leanings risked denominational censure. In 1842, a few popular Methodist preachers in New England and upstate New York reluctantly concluded that faithfulness to their Wesleyan principles demanded separation from the Methodist Episcopal Church and "the absorbing power of [its] overgrown episcopacy[1]." Orange Scott, an uneducated but commanding pulpiteer, began the exodus. He offered this explanation:

> We wish it to be distinctly understood that we do not withdraw from any thing essential to *pure Wesleyan Methodism.* We only dissolve our connection with Episcopacy and Slavery. These we believe to be anti-scriptural, and well calculated to sustain each other.

Scott's sympathizers formed the Wesleyan Methodist Connection, a society Scott described as "anti-slavery, anti-intemperance, anti-every-thing wrong." A vocal minority attempted to exclude members of secret societies. People felt strongly on both sides of this issue: across the nation, attitudes toward oath-bound societies defined political as well as moral boundaries. "The Masonic question seemed to involve us in the most trouble of anything that came before us," one early participant observed. Leading men like Orange Scott were Masons, but in time opponents of secret societies mustered a majority, and the Wesleyan Book of Discipline[2] decreed that joining or holding fellowship with secret societies was "inconsistent with

---

[1] Episcopacy is government by bishops. Wesleyans believed that Methodist polity enabled bishops to dictate policies contrary to John Wesley's teachings.
[2] The Book of Discipline explained the Wesleyans' polity and doctrine.

our duties to God." Otherwise, Wesleyan Methodists affirmed familiar Wesleyan teachings, a point they highlighted regularly in the pages of *The True Wesleyan.*

Shaped by its distinctives

In 1845, the Wesleyan Methodist Connection issued its first hymnal. It testified to the group's broad consensus with American evangelicalism, but a few section headings identified the "true Wesleyan" distinctives: Christian perfection, Christian warfare, Christian zeal, Christian fellowship, formal religion, family worship, love feasts, the Sabbath, anti-slavery, temperance, world peace, and backsliding. Stirring hymns on these subjects sustained identity, activism, community, and vision. Wesleyan Methodists were committed to Arminian[3] holiness with a keen sense of social justice, a hunger for authentic Christianity, and a taste for lay participation in all levels of church governance. (Meanwhile, growing dissension over slavery within the Methodist Episcopal Church led to a division of the parent body into separate northern and southern denominations in 1844, a rupture that lasted until 1939.)

When Rufus Lumry gathered Wheaton's Wesleyan Methodist congregation in 1843, the denomination he represented was still forming. No records of the Wheaton church's first twelve years survive except a list of pastors, some of whom served the small congregation only a few months. Their brief tenures illustrate how all forms of Methodism grew on the frontier. Preachers did not settle for long. Rather, they evangelized at every opportunity, pushed into new territory, served small gatherings on circuit, and recruited laypeople into leadership roles. When one preacher pushed on, another stepped into the gap. Two years after the Connection organized, Orange Scott visited Illinois and reported in *The True Wesleyan* that he found twelve settled

[3] Arminians believe that Christ died for all–"whosoever will may come."

Wesleyan Methodist preachers and ten itinerants at work; several "veterans" of the two-year-old Illinois field had moved on into Iowa. Like other Methodists, the Wesleyan Methodists relied on laypeople. They valued women's testimony, encouraged women's evangelistic work, believed in women's education, and mobilized youth for Christian social witness.

From the movement's inception, Wesleyan Methodists also affirmed a commitment to education and called upon the faithful to establish Wesleyan Collegiate Institutes "combining the advantages of literary and theological training." Their model was Oberlin College, a school in northern Ohio, where women and persons of color had full access and evangelical piety undergirded social progressivism. Wesleyan leaders assured their small constituency that an investment in education would be repaid in "the universal triumph of every benevolent enterprise." With other Protestants, they felt a moral and patriotic obligation to advance civilization and Protestant religion in the West, and they embraced education as a means to this end.

The Illinois Institute

The Illinois Wesleyan Conference met in Batavia in 1851 and authorized the planting of a school in the area that would eventually become Wheaton. Their plan included a school with two divisions: an academy that prepared students for college and offered vocational training, and a liberal arts college. Local citizens, who had high hopes for the still unincorporated settlement, welcomed the idea and offered generous incentives. Jesse and Warren Wheaton, the brothers for whom Wheaton was named, donated forty acres of land, and in December 1853, the Illinois Wesleyan Conference opened the Illinois Institute. Classes began in the basement of the school's new building while construction proceeded above. Enrollment grew from 140 students the first year to 270 the next: for the first several years, the vast majority enrolled in the preparatory academy rather than at the collegiate level. The Institute's early presidents served as pastors of the Wesleyan Connection as well. In 1854, the Wesleyan congregation began meeting in the Institute's chapel, described as a "long low-ceilinged room" on the first level of the school building.

Illinois Institute programs were open to women and men and to people of color. Not many African Americans lived in northern Illinois, but several enrolled, boarding in local homes and becoming part of the Wesleyan congregation. One was Mary Barker, who became a teacher in Quincy, Illinois; another was Edwin B. Sellers, a former slave, who went on to Andover Seminary and then moved to the South to serve as a Congregationalist home missionary among the freedmen.

Meanwhile, Jesse and Warren Wheaton took steps to bring the railroad through their property and to plat and incorporate the village of Wheaton. Enthusiastic friends of the Institute, the Wheaton brothers participated as well in the early Wesleyan congregation. The school that grew up around it provided the new village with a concentration of vocal citizens whose private faith expressed itself in clear expectations about social relationships and civic life.

The Wesleyan Connection remained Wheaton's largest church, even after the Methodist Episcopal Church (North) (now Gary United Methodist Church) and a Baptist congregation (now First Baptist Church) began meeting in town. Gratifying enrollments at the Illinois Institute showed that the school fulfilled a local as well as a denominational niche. Wesleyans shouldered the financial burden, but from the outset they partnered with Congregationalists for leadership in the local church and the Institute. Regular preachers over the first ten years included Wesleyans Milton Smith (who also preached regularly in nearby Danby), Joel Grennell, and William Kimball, and three men linked to Knox College in Galesburg, Illinois–Reuben F. Markham, Lyman Beecher Ferris, and the Institute's second president, Charles F. Winship. (In 1856, Winship became a Congregational missionary to ex-slaves at the famous Mendi Mission in Sierra Leone.) The Institute's first president, John Cross, worked under the American Home Missionary Society, a union of Congregationalist, Presbyterian, and Reformed Protestants. Oberlin professor George Clark was a noted evangelist and popular pulpit supply; the celebrated abolitionist Alexander McArthur also filled the pulpit of the Wesleyan Connection of Milton Township.

Each man was distinguished in his own way–as an abolitionist, an educator, an evangelist, a church planter, or an author. The original congregation was shaped by the Wesleyan Book of Discipline, but the Wesleyans partnered easily with Congregationalists. They shared a preference for congregational polity, commitment to education and evangelism, and a passion for the twin endeavors of evangelism and social reform. Most of them proudly aided the Underground Railroad. (Rufus Lumry ran for Congress on the Abolitionist Party ticket.) Yet despite their combined fervor for the gospel and the nation, they could not assure the financial success of the Institute or the church.

In the fall of 1856, Lucius Matlack, an experienced pastor, editor, and Wesleyan denominational leader, became president of the Institute and pastor of the Wesleyan Connection in Milton Township. The next year, nationwide business and bank failures accompanied a sharp economic downturn known as the Panic of 1857; national economic problems complicated the Institute's shaky financial situation. Matlack realized that the school could not continue as it was, and he entertained two options: dissolution or takeover. In May 1859, he offered the school to the Illinois Congregational Association with a request that the Association raise an endowment. The Association declined, but it appointed a committee to see what could be done. While the process inched along, Wheaton citizens rallied to meet immediate needs.

A timely visit

At a critical moment in July 1859, a peripatetic Congregational educator, pastor, and social activist named Jonathan Blanchard traveled through Wheaton en route to a speaking engagement elsewhere. The Illinois Institute and Knox College were connected in the 1850s, so Blanchard knew the Institute's predicament but believed it was worth saving. He addressed the Illinois Wesleyan Conference then in session in Wheaton, boarded with Institute president Matlack, and fielded questions about his potential interest in the Institute's presidency. He refused to commit himself, but the overture was timely. Blanchard's future was uncertain, and he had in hand several offers from colleges and congregations.

Late in 1859, Jonathan Blanchard agreed to take on the challenge presented by the Institute's financial predicament. He accepted an offer of $3,000 to become president of the Institute and to serve two years as pastor of the Wesleyan Connection in Milton Township. Blanchard acted without the official blessing of the Illinois Congregational Association (of which he was a member); when its committee finally met, however, it recognized the school's dire predicament and affirmed the process that had brought Blanchard to Wheaton without awaiting Association approval.

The terms under which Blanchard assumed leadership of the Institute and the pastorate of the Wesleyan Connection gave him the right to change the names of both, but demanded his promise to uphold the Wesleyan social witness, especially its testimony (or witness) against slavery. In January 1860, Blanchard began preaching as supply pastor of the Wesleyan Connection.

On February 2, 1860, the congregation acquiesced to Blanchard's wish to change its name to The Church of Christ in Wheaton. Blanchard personally affirmed the six Wesleyan testimonies that aligned the congregation with specific social views: opposition to slavery, secret societies, dancing, and gambling, and support for temperance and Sabbath keeping.

At the time, most northern Illinois Congregationalists favored these principles, and if the Wesleyans had not put them in place, Blanchard would certainly have done so for his own reasons. The congregation had dual affiliation with the Wesleyan Conference and the Congregational Association. The name of the Illinois Institute also changed: with the surrender of its original charter and the issuance of a new charter in 1861, the school became Wheaton College.

When the Congregationalist Jonathan Blanchard took charge of the Wesleyan Connection in Milton Township, the congregation accepted the fact that changes would follow in the church as in the college. Cooperative work with Congregationalists was not unusual for these early anti-episcopal Methodists. The Wesleyan Book of Discipline established the framework of congregational life, though, and the "original members" of the church were in the majority: there was no Congregationalist cohort waiting in the wings, though Blanchard immediately added Illinois Congregationalists to the Wheaton College Board of Trust (as it was then known). In fact, their impatience with the Methodist episcopacy attracted many Wesleyans to Congregational polity, and both denominations embraced core evangelical beliefs and cared deeply about shaping a Christian America. Differences in emphasis and style soon surfaced, though, and the conclusion of Blanchard's pastorate in 1862 made an amicable separation timely. On November 29, 1862, some of the original members officially withdrew to reconstitute Wheaton Wesleyan Church.

The Wesleyan Methodists had indeed shaped the original

congregation that was to become College Church. Under their Book of Discipline, it was revivalistic, Arminian, experiential, socially involved, and lay oriented. They gave The Church of Christ in Wheaton its distinctive character, especially its prominent social witness. Their robust hopes for the community and the nation persisted under Jonathan Blanchard, as did their firm commitment to holiness and revivalist evangelical piety. But Illinois Congregationalists had different roots and a different history, and these also mapped the congregation's future. If the Wesleyan Methodist story explains how the congregation came to be, Congregationalist connections clarify its ties to an older web of Protestant endeavors dedicated to Christianizing America and the world. Cooperation between Congregationalists and Wesleyans was one thing; replacing the Book of Discipline with a Congregationalist church manual was quite another.

The Illinois Congregationalists

By birth, upbringing, and education, Jonathan Blanchard belonged to a network of men and women with aggressive agendas for shaping a Christian nation. Blanchard's formative years corresponded with the heyday of New England Congregationalist activism in the old Northwest Territory—Ohio, Indiana, Wisconsin, Michigan, and Illinois.

New England young people with an eye to the nation's future stamped Illinois Congregationalism with a forward-looking character. In 1829, seven divinity students at Yale College publicly pledged their lives to gospel work in Illinois. Inspired by a student address sponsored by the Yale Society of Inquiry Respecting Missions, the men vowed to plant the New England Way—with its distinctive blend of religion and education—on the prairie. An article in the *Home Missionary Magazine* drew their attention to the Rev. John Ellis, a Congregationalist missionary raising funds to plant Illinois College in Jacksonville. At Ellis's ordination at Boston's Old South Church, the Rev. Elias Cornelius had charged him to "build up an institution of learning which shall bless the West for all time." Ellis was doing his best to realize that goal, and the Yale band of students caught the vision. One member wrote:

To think of the present number of immortal souls within our own country living on trial for an endless destiny is deeply affecting, and to think of their rapid increase in a situation where little or no light shines to invite them to the world of felicity or to warn them of that dark abyss to which they rapidly hasten is truly overwhelming.

Other bands of Congregationalists from New England schools followed the Yale example and planted Congregational institutions on the prairie, each institution characterized by the moral and spiritual hopes for the nation associated with contemporary religious revivals.

Quickened by revivals, New England Congregationalists had long looked westward with a lively sense of purpose. Already in 1812, Congregationalists had sent Samuel J. Mills (of Haystack Prayer Meeting fame) to survey prospects in the West. In Illinois he found five Baptist congregations totaling 120 members, six Methodist meetings adding up to 600 members, and no Congregationalists or Presbyterians. Mills's New England backers remedied that neglect by sending itinerants to "plunge into the wilderness, look up the people, preach, organize churches, and then go along." Meanwhile, New England Congregationalists formed the new nation's first foreign missionary society, the American Board of Commissioners for Foreign Missions (ABCFM, chartered

1812), helped establish the American Home Missionary Society (1826), and played leading roles in the American Bible Society (1816), the American Tract Society (1825), the American Sunday School Union (1824), and a long list of other voluntary societies chartered to spread the gospel and Protestant civilization at home and abroad.

Illinois Congregationalism did not derive exclusively from the labors of New England home missionaries, though. Individuals and whole communities of settlers also brought their religious preferences with them. Since thousands of New England citizens settled in northern Illinois, Congregationalist sympathies were widely evident. In fact, some newcomers were so eager to plant their "true religion" on the prairie that they organized themselves into Congregational churches before coming west. The Hampshire Colony Congregational Church in Princeton, Illinois, for example, dates its beginning to Northampton, Massachusetts, where it organized in 1831 to "promote the cause of Christ by planting religious institutions in the virgin soil of the west and aiding the cause of Christian education in its various departments." Its members moved to Illinois as a fully organized congregation with a clear purpose. Between 1836 and 1841, other New England Congregationalists purchased land, moved in groups, and established towns around Congregational churches—for example, Geneseo, Rockford, and Lyndon.

The Plan of Union encourages denominational cooperation

Another source of Illinois Congregationalism overlapped with home missions work. In 1801, Congregationalists and Presbyterians realized that the rapid settlement of the West presented an evangelistic and civilizing challenge of the first magnitude. They devised a Plan of Union to promote cooperation in the West. The Plan offered guidelines for church governance and pastoral leadership across denominational boundaries–addressing, for example, how problems might be adjudicated where a Presbyterian pastor served a predominantly Congregationalist membership. At the time, New England Congregationalists and Presbyterians differed on polity rather than doctrine, and the only alternative was competition in a vast and underserved region. Many congregations formed under the Plan of Union later faced unanticipated difficulties, however. Congregationalists complained that Presbyterians (who were generally a minority of church members) reaped most of the benefits of the Union, grumbling that Presbyterians "churned Congregationalist milk to make Presbyterian butter." Theological disputes elsewhere also exacerbated local tensions.

In 1837 a Presbyterian schism divided that denomination into New School and Old School factions. Old School conservatives frowned on the new directions in Congregational theology associated with Yale College and Hartford Theological Seminary as well as on the revivalist sympathies of New School Presbyterians. Attitudes toward slavery clouded the picture, too, with Old School Presbyterians more inclined than their New School counterparts to spurn abolitionism. Congregationalist leaders in New England, meanwhile, worried that the Congregational Way–with its reliance on consensus–might not be suited to the frontier, where diversity reigned. Some Illinois Congregationalists wanted to demonstrate that the New England Way had a future wherever biblical religion prevailed, while others lived with the tensions associated with the larger cooperative vision enshrined in the Plan of Union.

A genuine Midwestern identity

Early Illinois Congregationalists did not present a united front. Some (like the congregation in Princeton) organized themselves; others worshiped in churches that functioned under the Plan of Union; still others participated in a small Illinois Congregational Association and saw themselves as part of the web of Congregational churches that extended outward from New England. All Midwestern Congregationalists sat under the ministry of college- and seminary-trained pastors ambitious in their work and adamantly opposed to slavery. Evangelistic fervor marked all Illinois Congregationalists. After the Civil War, when Presbyterians withdrew from the Plan of Union, the situation favored the growth of the Illinois Congregational Association. Soon the Illinois Congregational Association was second only to Massachusetts in the number of Congregational churches; the New England Way was no longer a regional phenomenon–it thrived in the Midwest. Its educational institutions, home missionaries, and congregations offered continuity with the nation's past, but Midwestern Congregationalism also stamped its character on the national association. In fact, during the 1850s the New England Way was so successfully transplanted in the Midwest that it brought about a national Congregational identity.

The Illinois Congregational Association began modestly in May 1844 when nine men braved floods and "the sickly season" to meet in Farmington, Illinois, to "bind themselves more closely together" to evangelize the growing population. They united around the profession that "each particular church is vested by Christ with the right to choose its own officers and regulate all its internal affairs" and that "a credible evidence of conversion to Christ is a prerequisite to membership in his church." They declared themselves unequivocally opposed to slavery: "We believe that the holding of our fellow-men as property is an immorality in practice, and the defense of it is a heresy in doctrine." In 1844, the Illinois population approached 600,000; there were forty Congregationalist pastors and 2,432 members. In 1846, Congregationalists established the American Missionary Association (AMA), a denominational rather than a cooperative venture, to support strictly Congregationalist home missionary work. Jonathan Blanchard served the AMA as a vice president.

Jonathan Blanchard: "Born to Wrangle"

When Jonathan Blanchard became pastor of the Wheaton Wesleyan Church in February 1860, the politics of Congregationalist relationships in Illinois became part of that congregation's story. A New England Congregationalist by birth and education, Blanchard affiliated the congregation with the Illinois Congregational Association. That meant that The Church of Christ in Wheaton supported foreign missions through the ABCFM and home missions through the AMA or the Plan of Union's American Home Missionary Society. Church women participated in the vigorous efforts of the denomination's Women's Home Missionary Union and the Women's Foreign Missionary Society.

From the start, Jonathan Blanchard's uncompromising personality influenced the congregation's reputation in the Northern Illinois Association of Congregational Churches. "Jonathan Blanchard was born to wrangle and enjoy wrangling," the Illinois poet and historian Carl Sandburg noted. The force of Blanchard's personality from 1860 until his death in 1892 made Jonathan Blanchard a formidable figure in the development of The Church of Christ in Wheaton.

A native of Vermont (b. 1811) and graduate of Middlebury College (1832), Blanchard began divinity studies at Andover Theological Seminary, the school orthodox Congregationalists had established in 1809 as an alternative to Harvard. Two years later, Blanchard withdrew to lecture for the American Anti-Slavery Society. After an eventful year on the abolitionist lecture circuit in Pennsylvania, he decided to complete his theological education at Lane Seminary in Cincinnati.

The influence of Lyman Beecher

The attraction at Lane was Lyman Beecher, patriarch of the famous Beecher clan, then at the height of his fame. A son of Connecticut, Beecher graduated from Yale, where he participated in the early phases of the Second Great Awakening. As a pastor and public leader, Beecher promoted the mix of activities that described early nineteenth-century evangelicalism—revivals, voluntary associations, Protestant education, home and foreign missions, Sunday schools, congregational singing, children's choirs. In 1832, Beecher left a prosperous Boston church to accept a call to the presidency of Lane Seminary in Cincinnati, then the largest city in the West and home to growing numbers of westward-moving New Englanders.

Beecher intended to save the nation by saving the West, and Cincinnati, the gateway to the West, offered him a strategic advantage. Lane Seminary was a Presbyterian institution, but that did not deter the staunchly Congregationalist Beecher. The Plan of Union made it possible for Beecher and his future son-in-law, Calvin Stowe, to work for a Christian America there as well as anywhere. At Lane, Blanchard made connections that served him for the rest of his life.

Upon graduation from Lane, Blanchard married Mary Avery Bent, a teacher he had met on his Pennsylvania abolitionist lecture circuit. He was ordained in Cincinnati on October 31, 1838, in a service conducted by Lyman Beecher and Calvin Stowe. Blanchard had already accepted a call to Cincinnati's Sixth Presbyterian Church, a prominent New School congregation recently served by Asa Mahan, the new president of Oberlin College. In Cincinnati and surrounding towns, Blanchard lectured against slavery at every opportunity. In 1843, he attended the second World's Anti-Slavery Convention in London as a delegate from the Ohio State Anti-Slavery Convention.

There he met Hiram Kellogg, the first president of Knox College, who convinced Blanchard to promote the institution. Two years later, the trustees of Knox College invited Blanchard to replace Kellogg as president. The Blanchards' move to Galesburg at the end of 1845 was fraught with obstacles precipitated by their adamant refusal to travel on Sundays. Blanchard entered heartily into his new work, enthusiastically endorsing the Knox College model of a college associated with the life of a local congregation, and affirming the potential of Knox College for the small town of 130 families and for the state of Illinois.

The Knox College years

Galesburg took its name from its founder, George Washington Gale. A New York Presbyterian pastor associated with the conversion of evangelist Charles G. Finney, Gale and like-minded anti-slavery Presbyterians and Congregationalists established the town, church, and Knox College in 1837. Like many upstart Midwestern colleges, Knox had bleak financial prospects. The country was in economic turmoil, and when the Blanchards arrived in 1845, the eight-year-old college had as yet no graduates. Jonathan Blanchard proved to be an energetic and successful fund-raiser, preacher, teacher, and administrator. He traveled tirelessly, exploiting his connections in the Northeast to raise support, keeping in touch with influential acquaintances in Ohio, networking widely in Illinois, and taking outspoken stands on the issues of the day that kept his name in the press. His refusal to compromise on anything he saw as a moral issue brought him notoriety as well as applause. In all, he presided over thirteen graduation ceremonies at Knox College.

Blanchard's accomplishments were overshadowed by his deteriorating relationship with George Gale. Bitter public feuding between the town's two most prominent citizens brought into focus a fundamental weakness of the Plan of Union that governed Congregational and Presbyterian cooperation: the Plan could not guarantee at the local level the goodwill it affirmed– especially when uncompromising personalities intruded. At first, Gale welcomed Blanchard to town in part because Blanchard's experiences among both Congregationalists and Presbyterians made him an ideal candidate for a college and pulpit sup- ported by both. In time, though, Galesburg Presbyterians and Congregationalists took opposing sides on a growing num- ber of matters, including Jonathan Blanchard. Disagreements between Blanchard and Gale pitted Congregationalists against Presbyterians. The unhappiness (known locally as the "Blanchard Wars") came to a head in 1857 and ultimately cost Blanchard his job. Knox students (there were just fifteen in 1858) tended to be Blanchard partisans, and a few left Knox College with him.

The pivotal move to Wheaton

An intractable and fearless man, a gifted orator, and an expe- rienced pastor and educator, Blanchard came to Wheaton in 1860 with strong feelings against slavery, secret societies, alcohol, dancing, gambling–in fact, anything he thought dis- tracted people from pursuing God's Kingdom. His experiences in Galesburg strengthened his bent toward independency.[4] He considered the celebration of Christmas unchristian, regret- ted the recent popularity of the game of croquet, and scented Masonic conspiracies in any opposition to his views. At the same time, though, he boarded African American students in his own home and helped place them after graduation. People recognized in him a knack for leading young people, but he could also be brusque, opinionated, and uncompromising. In

[4] The word *independency* is a term that originated in the seventeenth century, referring to people who insisted that the seat of power resided exclusively in a local body–elders or congregation–and who rejected any check on that power, even in the form of advice.

Wheaton he again became the focus of dissension in the college and its related congregation.

Blanchard renamed the Wesleyan Connection of Milton Township as The Church of Christ in Wheaton because he considered the new name biblical and following the custom of New England college towns. In 1860 he brought The Church of Christ in Wheaton into the Illinois Congregational Association, where he became a vocal—and bothersome—proponent of anti-Masonry. He served as pastor of The Church of Christ for only the promised two years, but he set the congregation on its course and remained a prominent member until he died in 1892. By then, his actions had permanently split the church membership; his public criticism had placed obstacles in the paths of two distinguished Illinois Congregational clergy; and his behavior had caused his name and that of The Church of Christ in Wheaton to be dropped from the rolls of the Illinois Congregational Association. Blanchard's unwillingness to compromise invited the controversy that followed him wherever he went. He influenced the early course of the church more than did any other single individual.

Wesleyans, Congregationalists, and Jonathan Blanchard put their stamp on the congregation that became College Church. These formative influences situated the congregation within particular streams of American evangelicalism and shaped a spiritual and social legacy with enduring relevance.

The Church of Christ in Wheaton

The Church of Christ in Wheaton met in Wheaton College's chapel, a room in the main building (now Blanchard Hall) described as "long and low." In 1866, Wheaton College trustees authorized major renovations that were accomplished over the next six years. An early step involved raising the roof of the main building to create a spacious third-floor area to function as college chapel and church sanctuary. Designed to seat more than 400 people in traditional pews, the chapel served constituencies that had considerable overlap. During these early years, students at Wheaton College were required to attend Sunday morning worship at The Church of Christ unless they produced a parental note requesting permission to worship in one of the few other local congregations. College faculty featured prominently in the leadership of the church. Students knew their instructors outside the classroom as church elders, Sunday school superintendents and teachers, deacons, and church musicians.

The college provided the chapel rent-free to the church; in return, the Ladies' Benevolent Society of The Church of Christ furnished the space. During the 1860s, the pastor's annual salary was $1,000, payable quarterly and raised by subscription. Fund-raising presented a constant challenge, and the congregation tried one plan after another. For several desperate months, members designated a collector to encourage people to contribute—he was permitted to keep for himself 5 percent of what he collected. In August 1872, members voted to finance the entire church budget by renting pews. Prices ranged downward from $40 per year, and rents were due quarterly in advance.

Two weeks into the experiment, the church clerk reported that many pews had been rented. Promoters of the idea, meanwhile, anticipated complaints and promised to keep every third pew free. A Committee on Seatings (the only committee composed solely of men) allocated space. Pew rental continued into the early 1900s, though by then it accounted for only a small portion of the budget. (Assigned family pews persisted into the 1930s when church growth made them impractical; it is unclear just when rents were abolished.)

Other subscriptions were due quarterly, and a collector monitored payments. (The pastor's salary fell behind whenever giving lagged.) On Sunday mornings, a bell summoned the faithful to worship at 10:30 a.m. It rang twice, at 10:00 and again at 10:20 when it rang for ten minutes. For the last seven minutes, it was slowly tolled. When the tolling ended, all unoccupied rented pews were considered free. In the 1890s, as the membership grew and seats were at a premium, all seating opened when the tolling began.

The new chapel was dedicated on June 1, 1873. Invitations went out to a list of pastors and delegates who were summoned to meet for prayer before the service began. The dedicatory sermon was preached by the Rev. Lathrop Austin Taylor, pastor of the Congregational Church in Farmington, Illinois.

Following Congregational custom, members joined The Church of Christ in Wheaton by affirming a covenant. The Illinois Congregational Association approved each member church's requirements for membership; the documents varied by congregation but conformed to widely held general standards. In Wheaton, the Wesleyans' six testimonies were part of the Church Manual, and these avowals were not empty words. Read aloud at regular intervals on Sunday mornings, they were frequently the subjects of sermons. Failure to comply was cause for discipline, and The Church of Christ took discipline seriously. The church gathered when any member brought charges against another; everyone listened to both sides and then voted to continue or withhold fellowship. Disciplinary sessions generally opened with thirty minutes of prayer, or they followed the regular midweek prayer meeting. All members heard the testimonies of prospective members, too, and voted on receiving them.

Music's deep roots in the church

Professor Freeborn Garretson Baker directed the Church of Christ choir and led the congregational singing. A Wesleyan Methodist from New England, he had studied with Lowell Mason, the era's best-known American church musician. Mason introduced him to the new forms of music education, congregational singing, and European-style choral training that were beginning to shape a distinctive American congregational sound. Mason's protégés made much of the "fit" between texts and tunes. They arranged tunes, conducted children's choirs, and taught people to enjoy music. When Baker joined the faculty of the Illinois Institute in 1857, he was already a veteran teacher. In the same year, he was appointed an Institute trustee. In addition to his duties at the school and the church, he organized a community Mendelssohn Society (in the style of Boston's Handel and Haydn Society) to bring music to the wider community.

In 1868 Baker led a small committee that reviewed The Church of Christ's music and offered some recommendations. Like Lowell Mason, Baker believed that a large choir drawn from the congregation could effectively lead congregational singing and provide special music. He already had a small choir, but he worked to expand it. Baker invited the congregation to choir meetings to learn how to sing—he wanted the congregation to sing at least two full hymns in each service from *Hymns for the New Life*, compiled by Darius E. Jones, music director at Henry Ward Beecher's Plymouth Church in Brooklyn, a place famous for its congregational singing. Baker occasionally used set pieces—anthems or chants—on special occasions or as preludes. He laid down principles for music that the congregation has followed to this day: a large trained choir, energetic congregational singing, accessible tunes, a place for set pieces—all to "render this part of public worship attractive to man, acceptable to God, and profitable to the church."

Pastors Lewis, Millikan, Brewster, and Walker

In pastoral leadership, Blanchard's immediate successor was Congregationalist Edwin N. Lewis, who for two years added responsibility for The Church of Christ in Wheaton to his duties as pastor of a small Congregational church in nearby Stacy's Corner. Between 1862 and 1878, only two of the six pastors who served The Church of Christ were regularly installed. (Most were under contract, renewed at specific intervals.) The first was Silas F. Millikan, a promising young man whose pastoral leadership from 1864 commended him to the congregation. (Millikan's son, Robert, a student at Wheaton Academy, would receive the 1923 Nobel Prize for physics.) In October 1866, after a daylong session with an ordination council composed of pastors serving in the Illinois Congregational Association, Millikan was ordained at The Church of Christ and installed as its pastor at a special evening service. Jonathan Blanchard prayed the ordination prayer.

A year later, however, at the conclusion of a Sunday morning service, Wheaton College professor John Calvin Webster stood before the congregation to read a letter from Pastor Millikan. The pastor had learned that some in the church opposed his ministry. Millikan sought the advice of the members and offered to resign if his service was unwelcome. At a special business meeting, Jonathan Blanchard moved acceptance of the resignation, although it had not been submitted formally. A few weeks later, Millikan was gone, though not before a Congregational Association council expressed confidence in Millikan and scolded The Church of Christ for dismissing him in an irregular way. Records suggest that Blanchard instigated the criticism of Millikan. The affair was an early indicator of a power struggle that would soon divide the church.

In 1868, The Church of Christ endorsed Joseph Galloway, a recent graduate of the college, for work among the freedmen of Mississippi. This was the first commendation of a specific person for specific service. At Jonathan Blanchard's suggestion, meanwhile, the congregation invited the Rev. William Brewster of Cleveland to become its pastor. Like the church itself, Brewster had moved from a Wesleyan Methodist connection to Congregationalism. He edited a Wesleyan Methodist hymnal, but at the same time accepted an invitation to plant a church in a schoolhouse near Cleveland that served all nearby Protestants. The church thrived under the motto, "In essentials unity, in nonessentials liberty, in all things charity." Whoever acknowledged "Christ as master" was deemed "a brother," and moral agreement took precedence over intellectual unity. The congregation soon affiliated with Ohio Congregationalists, and Brewster transferred his credentials.

A month after accepting the call to Wheaton, Brewster took up his duties. In 1869, his daughter, Henrietta, became the congregation's (paid) organist. In 1870, a committee was formed to suggest books for the first Sunday school library. The congregation counted 212 members, who voted to concentrate their giving in specific ways: January and February, work among freedmen and other projects of the American Missionary Association; March and April, the American Christian Union; May and June, home missions; July and August, the American Board of Commissioners for Foreign Missions; September and October, Bible societies; October and November, education; the last half of November and December, opposition to secret societies.

Members met frequently to pray and conduct business. The Church of Christ was growing and evolving with Wheaton but was still small enough for everyone to participate in the decision-making process. There were regular monthly business meetings as well as special sessions, weekly prayer meetings, Sunday services, a weekly college prayer meeting attended by many church members, an occasional week of prayer, and other special services. Professor John Calvin Webster's diary for 1871 often described services using phrases like "a good number present" or "a good spirit prevailed."

Webster, professor of rhetoric and logic at the college since

1864, was a nationally known Congregational pastor and author. Prominent in the leadership of The Church of Christ, he took responsibility as well for a preaching station in nearby Lisle. Pastor William Brewster, meanwhile, became so enthusiastic about Wheaton College that the congregation released him for two months (with salary) in 1871 to raise $5,000 to liquidate college debt. That fall the Congregational Church in Geneva called Brewster to become its pastor, and Brewster moved on in October (though he continued to serve Wheaton College). The Church of Christ rolls listed 249 members. The congregation found its next pastor, James Barr Walker, on the Wheaton College faculty. An Oberlin College trustee, Walker was a poet, publisher, and editor with a long life of service behind him. He served the congregation as pastor until he reached his seventieth birthday in 1875.

Growing contentions and the Cynosure

During these years of membership growth and ministry expansion, various differences of opinion fed an undercurrent of discontent and criticism within the core membership. First, and most obvious to all, were differences of opinion about Jonathan Blanchard. He factored somehow in every clash of opinions. For one thing, Jonathan Blanchard's growing obsession with secret societies impacted the church and the college. In 1868 Blanchard became senior editor of *The Christian Cynosure*, the official organ of the National Christian Association. It proclaimed that Freemasonry (and whatever resembled it, from the Knights of Labor to the Grange to college fraternities) was inherently anti-Christian. Blanchard admitted no common ground between Christianity and the remotest tie to any oath-bound society. Each issue of the *Cynosure* featured detailed renunciations by former Masons (the authenticity of such renunciations was often disputed) and articles that either belabored the evils of Masonry or exposed Masons in the nation's pulpits.

At The Church of Christ, the testimony against secret societies meant that prospective members (who were questioned publicly by the assembled membership) were required to avow opposition to Masonry. Occasionally a former Mason who had long since abandoned lodge meetings but still held life insurance through the lodge applied to join the church (usually by transfer of letter). Did owning insurance through the Masons disqualify someone for church membership? Insurance was not readily available and was one of the advantages lodges offered. Church members wavered briefly on this point, but in the end they insisted that prospective members break every tie to any lodge: being a Christian meant trusting the future to God, not to insurance. Any dissent was dutifully logged, occasionally discussed, but always dismissed.

One feature of governance caused division too. A discussion of eldership on February 22, 1877, drew a crowd that Jonathan Blanchard described as the largest ever assembled at the college chapel. A substantial body of members had raised objections to the custom of ordaining elders, a practice instituted at the church by Blanchard. The objectors held that elders were ordained clergy; laypersons should not be set apart by the laying on of hands for that office. Increasing the number of elders, they insisted, "endangered the liberty of the people," and they pointed out that New England Congregationalists had dropped the custom of ordaining elders–a "remnant of aristocracy"–in the early eighteenth century. Those who objected to ordained lay elders proposed a committee of members, either occasional or standing, in their place. (At the time, the congregation had four elders and four deacons.)

After spirited discussion, members voted 55 for ordained elders, 49 against; changing the Manual required a two-thirds majority, so the vote failed, but it showed a deep division. Jonathan Blanchard aired the discussion in the *Cynosure* with the comment: "The Wheaton church Manual declares it to be a Bible church and not a denominational one, so it is bound by its solemn covenant to have Bible elders." What other Congregationalists did or did not do was simply irrelevant.

In 1875, Lathrop Austin Taylor, a seasoned veteran among Illinois Congregationalists, had accepted the pastorate of The Church of Christ. Like Millikan, he was formally installed in that office. A son of New England, Taylor had earned a reputation as a faithful pastor and a wise and gentle man. Regular revivals and steady growth had distinguished his prior pastorates. The former chair of the Illinois Association's Board of Home Missions, Taylor had also served a term as district superintendent of the national American Congregational Union. Now in his sixties, he worked for unity at The Church of Christ. Jonathan Blanchard, meanwhile, attributed any disharmony to Masonic conspiracies occasioned by his unyielding opposition to Freemasonry.

Confrontations with Jesse Wheaton and John Webster

As a case in point, Blanchard cited the recent actions of Jesse Wheaton, the man for whom the city was named, a trustee of Wheaton College as well as one of the school's most generous benefactors and a close personal friend of many Church of Christ members. A successful businessman, Wheaton invested in a project to build what was known as the "central block" of the city of Wheaton. When the Masons signed a lease for the second floor of a building in the central block, Jonathan Blanchard held Jesse Wheaton personally responsible: the lease was not a business transaction, but a betrayal from within.

Blanchard forced Wheaton's resignation as a college trustee and began griping in print about Jesse Wheaton's treachery.

Sometimes he named Wheaton, but even when he did not, his meaning was clear. Church members and the larger community naturally took sides—Jesse Wheaton was a Christian brother, their neighbor, benefactor, and friend. It was, after all, one thing to oppose oath-bound societies and quite another to allege that disagreements proved the existence of conspiracies. Unhappiness with the rigor of Blanchard's anti-lodge stance flared anew. Blanchard freely used columns in the *Cynosure* to make his case and to denounce his detractors.

College finances also riled tempers. Because the personnel of college and church overlapped, unhappiness in one circle crossed easily to the other. In the early days of many Midwestern colleges, supporters subscribed to particular funds that established faculty chairs. Interest from investment of the fund provided the faculty member's salary. In 1864, New England friends of John Calvin Webster raised support for his professorship at Wheaton College. When he joined the faculty, Webster was in his fifties and had completed twenty-five years as pastor of the First Congregational Church of Hopkinton, Massachusetts. The college had many pressing financial concerns, and Jonathan Blanchard asked Webster's permission to draw a small loan from Webster's fund. Webster acquiesced.

When Blanchard sought another loan, however, Webster declined, and Blanchard took funds without permission. Webster objected: In his view, the funds raised by his friends for his support should not be appropriated for other purposes. Furthermore, when the principal shrank, so did his salary. Blanchard believed that money donated to the college belonged to the college—asking Webster was a courtesy but not a requirement.

Several public exchanges finally brought months of bickering about college affairs into public view. Blanchard was accused of using "ungentlemanly language" before a mixed audience in the college chapel. On one occasion during a heated altercation on a Chicago-bound train, he struck fellow church member J. W. Chapman, who had confronted him about appropriations from Webster's fund. A lawyer on the train witnessed Blanchard's assault, and Blanchard appeared before a justice of the peace soon after and paid a three-dollar fine.

The next morning, an unrepentant Blanchard justified himself to the students and faculty assembled for chapel. Blanchard's son-in-law, H. L. Kellogg, another witness to the argument between the two men, brought charges against Chapman, accusing him before the church of slander and falsehood. A congregational meeting barred Chapman from fellowship until he apologized, but a majority of members refused to reinstate him when he did.

Confrontations about college affairs brought festering discontent about other things to the fore. At the end of the 1876 academic year, the board of trustees, acting on Jonathan Blanchard's recommendation, fired the popular professor Webster. Church members—and students—took sides: after all, Blanchard and Webster were the two most prominent men in the congregation and the college. In 1877 Webster brought charges against Jonathan Blanchard before the church. He accused Blanchard of slander—"falsely accusing me of conspiracy against yourself and the college by wantonly and dishonestly declaring that I am 'mentally and morally incompetent to be a guide to our youth'"—and of depriving him of his means of living "by unjustifiable and unscrupulous measures."

The congregation met at 7:00 p.m. on December 27, 1877, to consider the matter. "The mud was very deep," Blanchard recorded, but the chapel was nonetheless well filled. After prayer, Bible reading, singing, and the reading of the church covenant, Webster presented his case. Cross-examination of witnesses and the reading of student statements supporting Webster filled the hours until midnight. Blanchard's defense and Webster's response lasted until 2:00 a.m. As soon as they finished, a Blanchard partisan, the physician A. H. Hiatt, moved to acquit Blanchard. His motion passed by a vote of 67–26, and the meeting adjourned.

Ill will remained. For more than a year, Blanchard's disagreements with Webster and Jesse Wheaton's unhappiness with Blanchard had divided the church and community. Webster's supporters demanded a financial statement from the college. Blanchard claimed that several donors had come forward and enabled him to return the money borrowed from Webster's account, but proof was not forthcoming: one named donor even denied that he gave. In May 1877, a few citizens of Wheaton appeared at the annual meeting of the Illinois Congregational Association at Sterling and asked the Association to endow Wheaton College, take over its affairs, and remove Jonathan Blanchard from the presidency. Blanchard's leadership seemed to jeopardize the entire enterprise.

On June 7, 1877, the *Cynosure* noted another petition with 150 signatures insisting that Blanchard be removed from office. The petition arose from a group of about four hundred Wheaton citizens, some of whom were members of The Church of Christ. Predictably, Blanchard fumed: "The lodge, which is the head of the serpent and the seat of his wiles in every town is the source of these troubles." His detractors insisted that secret societies had nothing to do with their growing distaste for Blanchard.

A Motion for Dissolution

On Thursday evening, January 3, 1878, The Church of Christ members gathered in the college prayer room (or "lesser chapel") to discuss a proposal brought by fifty-three members to follow standard Congregational Association procedure and submit their disagreements to a specially constituted council of Congregational churches. As soon as the meeting came to order, an unexpected motion for an "amicable dissolution" of the church was given precedence. Jonathan Blanchard summarized the case for separation as follows: Abraham and Lot separated to avoid quarreling; Jesus withdrew from those who sought to destroy him; Paul separated from those who spoke evil of him; Christians are commanded to withdraw from those who walk in a disorderly fashion. The vote to disband was 57–23. Both sides agreed to worship together in the college chapel for the last time the next Sunday, January 6.

As that meeting was about to adjourn, some in attendance protested that the proposal to submit disagreements to a council had not even been considered. Blanchard responded that it was unwieldy: "It must come into the college chapel and disrupt the studies of between 100 and 200 students." And since the congregation no longer existed, it had no disputes to resolve. Perhaps more to the point, John Calvin Webster had strongly urged a council.

During this disruption, Pastor Lathrop Taylor stayed with the church–or, from Blanchard's perspective, left with the minority. Since the smaller group considered the dissolution illegal (and a political move to protect Jonathan Blanchard), they continued to use the name The Church of Christ in Wheaton. Blanchard immediately barred them from meeting on the campus. They found space to rent at the Universalist Church on Wesley and Main Streets and asked the Illinois Association to convene a council to advise them. That council, composed of twenty-two Congregationalist pastors and faculty from Chicago Theological Seminary, gathered at Wheaton Baptist Church in February 1878. It heard testimony, deliberated, and concluded in a published report that the dissolution of The Church of Christ was an illegal act. The church had not been dissolved by vote on January 3, because only a unanimous vote of members could dissolve a church. Members who were refraining from worship with the smaller group remained under its covenant and "were walking disorderly before the church and before the world."

The report ruled against Blanchard (who, one witness told the council, was "really the cause of the whole trouble you are inquiring into") and offered him a week to "show by public confession and restitution why the fellowship of this church should not be withdrawn from you." Blanchard retorted that the council had no authority over him since his new congregation had no charges against him. "His congregation," a council legal adviser quipped, consisted of "his family, his sons and their families, his sons-in-law and their families, the faculty of Wheaton College and their families," and students required to attend the church. Former pastor Millikan weighed in with the assertion that Blanchard's word could not be trusted "in any matter of controversy that touched his interests."

Another witness reminded the council that in 1870, five Chicago men, four of them clergy, described Blanchard as "a reckless slanderer of his brethren, or of a state of mind which relieves him of responsibility for his actions," a judgment reported in the *Chicago Tribune*. If they had looked back further, Blanchard's detractors might have discovered even earlier precedents for Blanchard's disregard for process. During his vitriolic exchanges with George Gale in Galesburg in 1857, a knowledgeable observer commented in the *Quincy Daily Whig* that Blanchard "violated the principles of ecclesiastical order and courtesy" and manifested "independency with a vengeance."

The College Church of Christ is formed

Although they may have been technically at fault, the larger group hardly missed a beat. On January 7, 1878, they reorganized as a new church and, to avoid confusion, took the name

The College Church of Christ. Lathrop Taylor's congregation, meanwhile, voted to become The First Congregational Church of Wheaton. Taylor, educated like Blanchard at Middlebury College and Andover Seminary, now retained his standing in the Illinois Association, as did his congregation. Jonathan Blanchard and The College Church of Christ, meanwhile, were expelled.

Lathrop Taylor scrupulously adhered to accepted Congregational practices. When a few people requested letters of dismissal in order to join College Church, Taylor refused with the observation, "We cannot transfer our members to its connection and be ourselves orderly." He offered instead a letter affirming good standing in First Congregational Church. Members of First Congregational Church rejected ordained eldership and dropped the Wesleyan Methodist language of "testimonies" against specific behaviors.

Forsaking the form of testimonies was one thing; abandoning the content was another. Lathrop Taylor, John Calvin Webster, and other prominent members felt strongly about maintaining the substance of the testimonies, but when the question came to vote, the congregation found it much easier to leave such matters to personal convictions than to agree on rewording the proscriptions. Taylor and Webster, among others, signed a lengthy protest that was included with the meeting minutes: they observed that no members used tobacco or alcohol; few countenanced dancing; few favored lodge connections of any sort. In fact, a solid majority affirmed what the congregation had held from its beginning in 1843.

The absence of the testimonies from the Manual brought a barrage of criticism from Jonathan Blanchard against Taylor and his church. It was so relentless that three months later, "stung by the criticism of the church as unprincipled," Lathrop Taylor announced that he would retire at the end of August when he would complete five years in this pastorate (counting from the time of his installation as pastor of The Church of Christ in 1875). In the first three years, he had failed to achieve harmony; in the last two, he endured the harsh criticism of people he had long esteemed as colleagues.

Nonetheless, Taylor guided a congregation through reorganization and maintained his reputation and standing. On January 2, 1879, he dedicated a new house of worship (built at a cost of $5,500) for First Congregational Church on the southeast corner of Seminary and Hale Streets. Steadying a congregation amid troubles and leading it toward a positive future demanded mature wisdom. Taylor played by the rules even when Blanchard opted for his own way.

Three principal actors in the separation–Blanchard, Taylor, and Webster–were Congregational ministers in their midsixties. Each had been born in New England and prepared for the ministry at Andover Seminary. They distinguished themselves in pastoral ministry and brought enormous potential to the college and its congregation. The united efforts of these mature men should have been extraordinarily fruitful. Their common commitment to Christ and his Kingdom compounded the sadness of the divisions in church, college, and community.

CHAPTER 2
DIRECTIONS

Onward, then, ye people, join our happy throng;
Blend with ours your voices in the triumph song!
Glory, laud, and honor unto Christ, the king;
This through countless ages men and angels sing.

SABINE BARING-GOULD, 1865

ON MONDAY EVENING, January 7, 1878, two church business meetings occurred in Wheaton a few blocks apart. The larger group met at Wheaton College, gathering with absolute confidence in their right to organize a new church, while the smaller meeting insisted that it assembled as The Church of Christ. The two groups had financial matters to settle and officers to elect. On that Monday night, both took decisive steps toward separate futures.

At the college, Jonathan Blanchard's son, Charles Blanchard, proposed steps for restructuring the church. He advised requesting the college chapel as meeting space; recognizing as members of the new church all prior members in good standing who so desired; retaining the Church Manual–which contained the covenant, the testimonies, and the principles of church polity; inviting elders and deacons who remained to continue to serve; appointing a committee to settle financial matters with the other congregation. This plan enabled the organization of a new body to move seamlessly forward. To avoid confusion, it took the name The College Church of Christ (CCC).

Members opted to wait until May to select a new pastor: supplying the pulpit presented no problem since the congregation included several clergy. President Blanchard promptly approved the request for use of the college chapel, and in the next few weeks, members contributed $437 to settle Lathrop Taylor's salary and the financial claims of his congregation. Taylor's congregation took the organ, and a subscription was raised to replace it.

In February 1878, members of the new College Church of Christ declined an invitation to participate in the Congregational council called at the request of First Congregational Church to rule on the differences between the two churches. "For ourselves," they asserted, "we need no Council." Lathrop Taylor's congregation had their "good wishes and prayers that God will amend whatever is amiss in our relations." When First Congregational Church attempted to follow the recommendations of the council, College Church responded with a lengthy protest. Language on both sides made clear that deep hurts persisted and that disentangling the congregations involved much more than reorganization or financial settlement. Neither congregation could flourish without acknowledging the right of the other to exist and prosper.

Pastor Charles Blanchard

In May 1878, College Church requested reinstatement by the Elgin Congregational Association, its local tie to the national body. After boycotting the council that examined the situation and ignoring its recommendations, the church now offered to cooperate in a special Association meeting to "examine the causes of our separation." Not surprisingly, the Association denied the request. The congregation next selected Charles A. Blanchard as its pastor (the vote was 34-3, with one vote each for three other ordained men in the congregation). On Wednesday, June 5, 1878, a council composed of nine area pastors, six of them Congregationalists in good standing in the Association, one independent, one Free Methodist, and one Wesleyan, plus Jonathan Blanchard, examined Charles Blanchard and approved his ordination.

Charles Blanchard took 1 Corinthians 9:18 as his "ministry verse": "What is my reward then? Verily that, when I preach the gospel, I may make the gospel of Christ without charge, that I abuse not my power in the gospel." The same council examined and ordained Charles Blanchard's brother-in-law, W. H. Fischer, on the same day. Already a popular college faculty member, Fischer had a heart for evangelism. The son of German immigrants, he reached out to the area's growing immigrant population and occasionally filled the pulpit at College Church.

So began a five-year pastorate that set The College Church of Christ on its future course. Charles Blanchard was his father's longtime assistant and a faculty member at Wheaton College. He knew the past and understood the interrelated circles of college, church, and neighborhood. More conciliatory than his father, he brought a new style of leadership at a difficult time. Old disagreements and personality conflicts sometimes flared. Blanchard's inability to reunite College Church with the Congregational Association frustrated him, but in general the church moved steadily forward.

Newcomers with no connections to past troubles as well as a changing mix of students helped the church grow, though in most years the church dismissed to other congregations almost as many members as it received. Wheaton's population was mobile (often westward moving), and people who transferred membership extended the congregation's visibility and furthered contacts with evangelicalism elsewhere. Despite the rupture with the Illinois Association, the overwhelming majority of transfers in and out continued to be to or from Congregational churches. College Church remained firmly ensconced in Congregationalist networks.

The cooperation of several ordained clergy associated with Wheaton College and College Church made Charles Blanchard's pastorate possible. Charles Blanchard was an experienced pulpit supply and had cultivated his formidable oratorical skills as a lecturer in the anti-Masonic movement, but he had limited pastoral experience and considered himself more a teacher than a preacher. He read his sermons from carefully prepared manuscripts. Most often, he took a theme from a single verse of Scripture. "I was in the Spirit on the Lord's day" from Revelation 1:10, for example, became a meditation on proper observance of the Sabbath.

"We have fine audiences every Sabbath day," his wife, Ellen, wrote in 1879 to her mother-in-law, Mary Blanchard, traveling in California with her husband, "and Charlie has something good for all each time no matter how much other work he has to do." Charles Blanchard confided to his father at the same time, "Matters in college and church seem running smoothly along. We have not a great interest in the one needful thing. The meetings are all well attended and yet there is not a breaking of the ice." He longed for renewal and held that desire before the congregation. A few years later, he expressed his yearning for revival with another metaphor: "I long for 'the fire to burn.'"

A milestone in 1879 was the installation of the new organ. It cost $115, an amount raised in small donations over many months. Ellen Blanchard commented, "I like its looks and tone much better than the one we had before the division." In some years, more than a third of the modest (often as little as $40) music budget paid for college students to pump the organ. (By 1889, the congregation was again raising money for an organ– this time it set its sights on a quality pipe organ.)

In 1882, in cooperation with the Wesleyan Methodists, Wheaton College provided space for a Wesleyan Theological Seminary. Illinois Wesleyans all along maintained an interest in the college: their annual conferences sent good wishes, and during the troubles of 1877, some talked of resuming an active role in college governance. The new seminary president, the Rev. Lemuel Nathan Stratton (a graduate of the Illinois Institute class of 1860 and a Wesleyan who became a Congregationalist), took a prominent place at College Church. A tireless church planter, pastor, and temperance activist, his travels and speaking engagements brought new attention to the college and congregation. An invitation to address the Chautauqua Assembly in 1883, for example, put Stratton in one of contemporary Protestantism's most famous venues, a summer gathering of fifteen to twenty thousand people in earnest about "lived Christianity."

Despite its promise, though, a denominational seminary was not a natural "fit" at a nondenominational college, and at the end of the decade, the seminary closed its doors. College Church felt the loss; the seminary had reinvigorated personal ties with Wesleyan Methodists that gradually diminished when it closed. The small group of male and female seminarians attended College Church and participated in its community outreach. Mrs. Stratton set the example by becoming the energetic president of the Wheaton chapter of the Women's Christian Temperance Union (WCTU), while her husband was a popular pulpit supply.

A Change in Pastors and College President

One of the names on the roster of both college and church during Charles Blanchard's pastorate was that of the Rev. Albert

J. Chittenden. An experienced pastor and onetime Greenback Party candidate for the Colorado governorship, Chittenden preached at College Church in January 1881, taking his text from Matthew 11:12: "The kingdom of heaven suffereth violence, and the violent take it by force." The emotional exuberance of local Free Methodists was then the talk of the town, and Chittenden cautioned: "The violence which takes the kingdom of heaven is not that which pounds the pulpit, stamps the floor and yells in the ears of the Almighty. But even as our loving is to be done with all our might, so nothing less than all our strength is sufficient for the purpose of any Christian function. Our Christian duties absorb too little of our time and strength."

The congregation warmed to Chittenden's ministry, and his preaching helped the hard-pressed Charles Blanchard to meet his responsibilities. In 1880, ill health forced Blanchard to take a leave of absence, and friends provided an extended trip to Great Britain. On his return, he found it necessary to spend much of 1881 soliciting funds to liquidate the college debt. Then in mid-1882, Jonathan Blanchard handed over to his son the presidency of Wheaton College. He promised the assembled convocation, "You will find him a much sweeter man than I am. He does not take after me. He takes after his mother in his disposition. I expect great things from him through the blessing of God."

With increasing responsibilities at the college, Charles Blanchard was forced to resign his pastorate. Preparing two sermons each week while teaching five hours every school day and fulfilling his administrative duties presented "altogether too heavy" a load. "I laid down the charge of the pulpit, to the apparent regret of the congregation," he recorded in his diary.

Charles Blanchard did not preach as regularly as most College Church pastors did, but he nonetheless guided the congregation with a sure hand during its difficult transition, and he continued to do so as its most influential member until his death in 1925. He yearned palpably for unmistakable signs of corporate spiritual quickening and kept that longing before the membership. He networked widely in Congregational and broader Protestant circles and gained perspective on developments in American Protestantism. He could be counted on to bring any sermon around to the testimonies, an emphasis that heightened sensitivity to cultural trends and local laws while keeping the congregation's earliest commitments prominent. And Charles Blanchard did all he could to rebuild cordial relationships with the Congregational Association. Once Jonathan Blanchard had made his point in 1877 and 1878, the leadership of College Church did not opt to remain independent but rather valued membership in a cooperative body.

The ongoing presence in the congregation of Jonathan and Charles Blanchard and their large extended families may have complicated the work of succeeding pastors. Chittenden, for one, proved less popular as pastor than as pulpit supply: within a few years, rumblings of dissatisfaction again pointed toward leadership change. He resigned in 1889 after a seven-year pastorate that was the longest to date in College Church's history. The Chittendens moved on to oversee a new Congregational Academy in Grandview, Tennessee, that served a growing population in the northeastern "mineral belt" of that state.

Prior to Chittenden's resignation, College Church reentered the Illinois Congregational Association. A series of conversations in 1888 chaired by the Rev. E. P. Goodwin, pastor of Chicago's influential First Congregational Church, paved the way. The Association required a letter of apology from Jonathan Blanchard for slandering a brother minister, a requirement that Blanchard fulfilled with objections.

Several short pastorates

Short pastorates would be the rule at College Church for the immediate future. When Chittenden left, the congregation turned to James Brewer, a seasoned pastor who had retired to Wheaton. Brewer agreed to help College Church through its pastoral transition by serving one year (1890–1891). From June 1894 through December 1898, one of the congregation's own, William H. Chandler, served as pastor. An ordained Congregationalist, Chandler was a leader in the new Christian and Missionary Alliance and like Charles Blanchard, he was a friend of Alliance founder A. B. Simpson. Chandler's multiple interests made a long pastorate impractical.

Yale-educated Edwin S. Carr (1899–1902) taught part-time at Wheaton College and was popular with students, but he resigned because he objected to how the rigid policy on lodge membership was enforced. Carr's successor, Walter Ferris (1902–1905), was the son of one of the preachers who had served the congregation before Jonathan Blanchard's arrival in 1860. (Ferris was a cousin of George Washington Ferris who invented the Ferris wheel, a landmark attraction at the 1893 World's Columbian Exposition in Chicago.) Between 1906 and 1909, William Evans tried unsuccessfully to combine teaching at Moody Bible Institute with the pastoral duties at College Church.

The congregation released most of these short-term pastors with regret and followed their subsequent work through Congregationalist periodicals and conferences. In some ways, though, continuities were as notable as frequent changes. Most pastors came from the Northeast, had similar educational backgrounds, moved within the same circles, and were formed by the same Congregational values. Despite short tenures, the denominational network provided a measure of stability.

Healing the broken relationship

Locally, the relationship between College Church and First Congregational Church slowly improved. In November 1904, ninety members of both congregations met for a union prayer meeting at the First Congregational Church. College Church often participated in union services, but this was the first at which these two congregations came together–twenty-six years after the division–and First Congregational took the initiative. A few weeks later, College Church reciprocated. Soon Wheaton College professors were occasionally supplying the First Congregational pulpit. Both congregations at last put the past behind them. In 1910, First Congregational Church opted to become First Presbyterian Church of Wheaton, the first Presbyterian congregation in Chicago's western suburbs.

Resolving issues with the denomination and with First Congregational Church freed College Church to flourish in new ways. Its ministries expanded as its membership grew. In the years leading up to World War I, College Church was shaped by its place in the larger stories of the Wheaton community, Wheaton College, denominational life, Protestant trends, and evangelical impulses.

The Wheaton Community

As the town of Wheaton grew, College Church took its place as one among a growing number of churches. No longer the only church in town–or the largest–it counted among its members some of the area's early settlers and maintained a vital interest in local affairs, which manifested itself in many ways.

For one thing, College Church cooperated with other churches in united endeavors for evangelism and social witness. Union services were common events in small-town America where polity preferences rather than sharp doctrinal disputes typically separated Protestants. Congregationalists, Methodists, Baptists, and Presbyterians had much in common, and union services provided opportunities to bear witness to their shared faith. In Wheaton, union services generally included CCC and the Methodist, Baptist, and Episcopal churches, and occurred most often on Sunday evenings, when they replaced regular gatherings in the respective churches.

For many years, the services became a Wheaton summer tradition: well into the 1930s, Protestants gathered on summer Sunday evenings on the lawn of Wheaton Community High School. The Baptist, Methodist, Congregational, Episcopal, and (later) Lutheran pastors preached in turn, and visiting evangelists provided variety. In inclement weather, College Church's spacious sanctuary often provided meeting space. When well-known temperance lecturers, YMCA workers, or Sunday school promoters were in town, special union meetings were arranged. Everyone united for community events like the annual high school or college baccalaureate services. Community-wide revivals, college-based special services, or revival meetings in any one congregation might become an occasion for other churches cancelling services to join in. In the summer of 1893, union meetings for the promotion of holiness generated so much interest that Wheaton congregations organized regular Sunday afternoon union prayer meetings.

CCC members also joined in community-wide temperance work. CCC women were active in the Wheaton chapter of the WCTU. The congregation promoted the efforts of the DuPage Sunday School Association, and CCC people helped to staff mission Sunday schools in places like Roselle, Bloomingdale, Lisle, York Center, Plano, and Winfield.

Maintaining an upstanding reputation

The prominence of the testimonies in shaping College Church kept members alert for violations of local ordinances. Church records preserve glimpses of energetic opposition to boxing, gambling, and Sabbath breaking as well as to lodges. In 1895, members went on record against a racetrack opened north of town. In May 1906 the congregation discussed a resolution opposed to Sunday baseball games that asked the Wheaton News Company "not to send to our homes dodgers [circulars] soliciting our children to Sabbath desecration." On May 23, 1906, members voted to send to the Wheaton newspapers and to the railway officers of the Aurora, Elgin, and Chicago Electric Road copies of a petition requesting Christians to abstain from Sunday travel and asking the company to "allow its employees to obey God's law."

The congregation often commended the Wheaton city council's efforts to enforce ordinances against Sabbath breaking, liquor selling, gambling, and other evils. Vigilance in public affairs characterized members of CCC, and they were quick to act to uphold their values. Occasionally, they petitioned their representatives in Springfield, Illinois, or in Washington, D.C. Many CCC members were politically involved, and the congregation easily mustered the votes to pass resolutions about public affairs.

Perspectives on national affairs

Along with other local congregations, College Church marked national events and responded to natural disasters. Patriotic anniversaries were community-wide religious as well as civic occasions, with prayers, hymns, and addresses as well as parades and picnics. President James Garfield's death from an assassin's bullet in 1881 was the topic for Sunday morning and evening sermons at CCC the next week. Charles Blanchard had the morning service to himself, but in the evening four orations, including one by Jonathan Blanchard, interpreted the assassination as a judgment of God for national sins. When Ohio River floods devastated southern Ohio in 1884, the church took a special offering for the "Ohio Sufferers." When the tumultuous Pullman Strike impoverished railroad workers' families in 1894, CCC sent an offering to "the Pullman poor." In 1909, a disaster at the Chicago, Milwaukee & St. Paul Railroad Coal Mine in Cherry, Illinois, entombed 259 men. CCC promptly contributed to the relief fund. A few weeks later, another offering expressed sympathy for the tens of thousands of victims of an earthquake and tidal wave in southern Italy. An offering for the poor, taken at each Communion service, relieved the needs of members or local people in dire straits.

When the Illinois Supreme Court banned Bible reading in public schools in 1910, the College Church pastor read a resolution of protest at the Sunday morning service, and the congregation voted to accept it. In 1911, the church mailed a resolution (again passed during the Sunday morning service) to William McAdoo demanding that the United States nullify its 1832 treaty with Russia because of the country's violations of religious freedom. McAdoo (later Secretary of the Treasury and Woodrow Wilson's son-in-law) led a New York–based movement for abrogation and testified before Congress as part of the process that ended the treaty. On Sunday, February 9, 1913, the congregation agreed to send a telegram to Illinois senator Shelby Cullom urging support for a bill that prohibited shipment of liquor through dry territory. College Church members regarded such vigilance as a Christian duty.

When Jonathan Blanchard ran for the presidency on the American Party ticket in 1884, national political debates had special resonance in Wheaton, though church records preserve no comments on that tumultuous election. Solid support for temperance meant that Democrats were scarce, noted the college newspaper, *The Wheaton Record*, but most people doubted that the overtly Christian reform agenda of the National Christian Association (expressed through the American Party) constituted a viable platform for a national political party. The *Record* recognized that on some matters, consensus did not prevail in Wheaton, but "a few heroic souls among us will stand on the platform called 'American' and vote for principles which they have faith to believe will one day prevail in this country."

Of the more than 10 million votes cast that November, candidates of the four largest parties received all but 3,576: Jonathan Blanchard won only a small share of these. He was never a serious contender, but candidacy gave him the opportunity to belabor his favorite public issues. As the election approached in 1884, Charles Blanchard's wife, Ellen, wracked with illness, politicked from her deathbed, soliciting from her visitors their promise to cast their votes for specific candidates who upheld her values.

College Church took its place in the community of Wheaton. Its members made good citizenship a priority. They also expressed their solidarity with other local Protestants by frequently worshiping together and working together for the public good.

Wheaton College

College Church's connections to Wheaton College also contributed to its distinct character. The two institutions shared not only space but constituency. Faculty, staff, and students worshiped at the church, and the church used college space—not only the chapel, but also the prayer room and public areas of the women's dormitory. The congregation installed a basic kitchen in the dormitory to facilitate its social functions, and the church furnished and updated the chapel. In 1896, CCC paid for the installation of electricity in the chapel, and every few years it purchased chapel hymnals. The college, meanwhile, used the church's organ for recitals and lessons. College special services and weekly prayer meetings on Tuesday evenings relied on the same people who attended the church prayer meetings on Wednesdays. Baccalaureate always replaced the CCC Sunday morning service, and other college events regularly found a place on the church calendar too.

The college brought to the church and the larger community special religious services, academic lectures, debates, concerts, entertainment, and other events that enriched the cultural life of the community. In the fall of 1910, it began holding annual eight-day Bible conferences featuring guest speakers, with mornings devoted to Bible teaching, afternoons to missions, and evenings to evangelism. Before World War I, college faculty always included several ordained Congregationalists who played leading roles in the church as elders, meeting chairmen, delegates, and pulpit supply. Few congregations had so many experienced preachers among their membership. Devoted to public ministry and service, these men influenced church priorities and activities.

The college faculty and student body often supplied church musicians—choir directors, organists, vocalists—as well as Sunday school workers. Before 1900, the vast majority of college students came from rural Illinois, and the student body shared the Protestant ethos of small-town America: Wheaton was familiar—a growing community marked by Christian values expressed through congregational and civic life. Some college students had been former slaves, and others came to the school because of the vitality of Congregational and Presbyterian missionary work in the Ottoman (or Turkish) Empire.

The Congregational Association

Denominational affiliation influenced all aspects of CCC. The congregation's Manual–containing its membership covenant and governance procedures–conformed to denominational expectations and was approved by the Illinois State Association before the church affiliated. CCC paid dues to the local arm of the State Association (five cents per member) and an annual "tax" to the Illinois Association. Members sent voting delegates to Association meetings as well as to national Congregational assemblies. A large percentage of CCC giving went to Congregational benevolences. The congregation took its turn hosting Association business sessions or the quarterly daylong meeting of the Fox River Congregational Club, a social event open to ministers and members of the forty area Congregational churches.

Statewide and local Congregational associations filled spiritual and social functions. Member churches designated delegates to church dedications, formed councils for discipline, and examined candidates for ordination and then ordained them. Prominent Illinois Congregationalists served as Wheaton College trustees, and during the divisions of 1878-88, some took initiative to plead with the Blanchards to make the first move toward reconciliation.

In some ways, the Congregational associations constituted a caring spiritual community united around nurture, social witness, and gospel proclamation; in other ways, the associations functioned as political entities through which denominational interest groups promoted particular causes. In Jonathan Blanchard's case, the cause was opposition to lodges. His last public utterance was a memorial to the Illinois Association (convening in Rockford the day he died in May 1892), reminding them that thirty years before they had gone on record against secret societies: "The appalling fact remains that we have on our hands a giant's task unfinished." After Blanchard's death, the local Association's outright opposition to lodges diminished notably.

The Preparatory Lecture

Congregational customs governed CCC's practices of church membership, baptism, and Communion. Saturday afternoon meetings that featured a "Preparatory Lecture" by the pastor preceded bimonthly Sunday morning Communion services. The Preparatory Lecture generally concluded with the public examination of applicants for membership, and those the congregation voted to receive were welcomed as members on Communion Sunday.

Covenantal language shaped the understanding of membership: people did not simply "receive the right hand of fellowship" but were "received into covenant relations with the church." Membership covenants reached back to the English Reformation when the first Congregationalists rejected state churches and viewed congregations as covenanted communities of baptized believers. Historically, when people "owned" a church covenant, they did more than make a profession. They entered publicly into spiritual rights they already possessed in a way that touched the core of their being.

The custom of the Saturday Preparatory Lecture preserved (in much modified form) a classic feature of the Reformed tradition where preparation for Communion Sunday once demanded rigorous and prolonged self-examination, confession, restitution, and pastoral visitation. Admitting people "into the communion of this congregation" (or, "inviting them publicly to own the church covenant") and baptizing those who joined on profession of faith just before the celebration of the Lord's Supper were theologically significant practices echoing ancient Christian tradition.

Baptism, membership, and Communion were closely associated: baptism preceded "owning" the church covenant upon profession of faith or reception by letter (which involved "owning" a slightly different covenant). Baptizing and receiving members on Communion Sunday gave special significance to the Communion service. (Surviving records intimate that participation in Communion may at times have been limited to members, linking baptism, membership, and Communion as the early church did.) Keeping church records was a demanding task with its own set of rules. People transferred in by letter from specific congregations, and they moved on with a letter of recommendation to a particular church.

Early Missionary Activity

Denominational affiliation also linked CCC to an international body of believers and invited its participation in Congregationalist efforts at home and abroad. As one of the oldest American denominations and with a membership concentrated in New England, Congregationalists were among the first to address the religious challenges of a new and growing nation. Their work in home and foreign missions was legendary. The American Board of Commissioners for Foreign Missions (ABCFM) was the nation's oldest missionary society, with preaching stations, schools, and hospitals around the world. Congregational home missionaries, meanwhile, worked especially among Mormons, African Americans, and Asian immigrants. The Congregational Women's Board mobilized women to support missionary work to and by women—"women's work for women." A Congregational Church Building Society allocated funds to needy congregations. A publishing society provided denominational literature. CCC contributed at least annually to each of these ministries, and in doing so, it became directly involved in some of the world's most troubled areas.

One such place was the Turkish Empire, an ancient entity that collapsed after World War I. In 1900, the ABCFM had some 100 congregations and 140 missionaries in the empire in addition to hundreds of national workers and thousands of Christians, all of whom faced danger on a daily basis. ABCFM's work among the Armenian population was particularly fruitful, and periodic Turkish atrocities directed against Armenians elicited protests from the West. The first two missionaries supported individually by CCC came to Illinois from different parts of the Turkish Empire to be educated for Christian ministry.

One was George H. Filian, the first commissioned missionary so designated in church records (May 31, 1882). Filian joined College Church in the spring of 1882, and after examination by a council of area pastors, he was ordained at College Church and commissioned for service in the Turkish Empire. An Armenian who was born in Antioch, Filian returned to Turkey under the ABCFM. He pastored the Constantinople Evangelical Armenian Church and then accepted a call to the Evangelical Armenian Church in Marsovan, a city with a vibrant Protestant witness. ABCFM schools such as Anatolia Theological Seminary and large boarding schools for hundreds of girls and boys, dozens of ABCFM missionaries, and thousands of Armenian Protestants made Marsovan, nestled in a picturesque valley near the Black Sea, a strategic center for ABCFM gospel work.

When Marsovan's growing congregation needed a larger sanctuary, Filian returned to the United States to raise money. Filian's successful fund-raising made him a target in the unsettled religious and political affairs of the decaying Turkish Empire. The government banished him as a revolutionary, and he returned to the United States to expose Turkish atrocities against Armenians. Soon after Filian was banished, the Turkish government burned down the ABCFM girls' school and massacred some three thousand Marsovan Christians. Filian documented the cruelty that accompanied Sultan Abdul Hamid's relentless campaign against his Armenian subjects. Filian moved to a growing Armenian enclave in Fresno, California, and became pastor of the Armenian Presbyterian Church there.

Another missionary on CCC's earliest list was an 1873 graduate of Wheaton College, Anastasios Zaraphonithes. A native of Andros in the Greek archipelago, Zaraphonithes enrolled in Wheaton as a special student and boarded at the Jonathan Blanchard residence. After finishing at Wheaton, he graduated from Union Theological Seminary in New York and then studied medicine at Long Island College in Brooklyn. In 1877, he became a United States citizen, married an American, and was ordained a Baptist minister. In 1878, he returned to Greece, where he served ten years as a medical missionary in Andros and Smyrna. After further studies in the United States and a second term in Greece (1892–1903), he settled permanently in the United States to work among Greek immigrants.

W. C. Cooper, "our pastor in Turkey"

Filian and Zaraphonithes gave CCC its first direct contact with Turkey–they were nationals who came to the United States for education and returned home to evangelize, rather than Americans who turned their sights toward evangelism abroad. The congregation's most sustained link to the empire, though, came through its embrace of William C. Cooper, a Wheaton College graduate who became an ABCFM missionary to Salonika and Bulgaria. College Church members referred to Cooper as their pastor and paid his full salary. He was pictured on the weekly church bulletin opposite a photo of the current CCC pastor; the caption identified him as "our pastor in Turkey." When Cooper married, CCC sent a gift; when the family returned on furlough, CCC provided an apartment; monthly personal letters, duly noted in the minutes, kept Cooper abreast of CCC news; when a former pastor traveled abroad during World War I, CCC authorized funds for a visit to its pastor, W. C. Cooper.

The relationship was unprecedented, but Cooper did extraordinary work at a strategic time and place. When Muslim Turks were overwhelmed by Greeks and Bulgarians during Balkan unrest, Cooper took charge of Western relief; he headed the Thessalonika Agricultural and Industrial Institute and directed the work of national colporteurs. In the years leading up to World War I, some considered Salonika the new capital of the Turkish Empire, and Cooper's efforts in this strategic center commended him to American supporters. A witness to the slaughter, pillaging, and reprisals that decimated parts of the Balkans in 1912–1913, Cooper worked with the Red Cross and other agencies to relieve suffering, evangelize, and teach. After World War I, he and his family took up missionary work in Bulgaria.

Missions at home

Stateside, CCC contributed to both denominational home missionary work and to particular independent missions. After the Civil War, Protestant home missionaries of all denominations poured their energies into evangelism among Mormons. Congregationalists planted the first Gentile congregation in Salt Lake City and devoted considerable resources to education. In 1890, forty-two Congregationalist home missionaries were under appointment to Utah, and 2,500 Utah children attended free Congregationalist schools. In addition to its contributions to the funds that underwrote these efforts, CCC regularly supported Mormon evangelism through agencies like the interdenominational Utah Gospel Association. When the Utah legislature elected

Mormon apostle Reed Smoot to the United States Senate in 1903, CCC petitioned the Senate not to seat him.

Assistance to former slaves claimed a regular share of the CCC budget too. In the 1870s, the congregation commended Joseph Galloway for this work; in the 1890s, gifts supported an up-and-coming African American preacher and social activist as well as Congregationalist missionaries in New Iberia, Louisiana; in 1913, W. T. Holmes, president of the Congregationalist Tougaloo University in Jackson, Mississippi (established in 1871 to educate African Americans), filled the CCC pulpit. In such ways, Congregationalists attempted to improve prospects for former slaves–education, evangelism, and job training claimed most of their attention. Closer to home, CCC contributed to the African American Second Baptist Church in Wheaton and welcomed the occasional African American Wheaton College students.

In practice, the church's Women's Missionary Society took responsibility for much of the congregation's day-to-day missionary program. Each Congregational church had its Women's Missionary Society, networked through a monthly publication prepared by the denomination's Women's Board. Society members studied the cultures in which Congregational missionaries labored, corresponded with missionaries, and sent barrels of goods to supply their needs. A mounting sense of solidarity among women characterized the thriving late-nineteenth-century women's missionary movement in which College Church participated. Foot binding in China or seclusion of women in India or Turkish violations of women and children summoned them as women to do everything they could for their victimized sisters.

Women in Ministry

Congregational affiliation impacted more than polity or patterns of giving and ministry. It also connected College Church with those who made room for women in ministry. The Illinois Association included a few ordained women pastors or evangelists. During Charles Blanchard's pastorate and then during his college presidency, women occasionally preached from the chapel pulpit. In 1883, Jennie Smith, a noted evangelist among employees of the Baltimore and Ohio Railroad and the national superintendent of the Railroad Department of the WCTU, spent a week in ministry at the church and college. That same year Frances Townsley, a member of the college class of 1870, held a week of special services open to college and congregation. An ordained Northern Baptist pastor and evangelist, Townsley was a guest in the Blanchard home, and Charles Blanchard commented, "For a woman to have so gained the high opinion of her fellow-laborers in ordination speaks for itself."

Church records preserve the names of women missionaries who occasionally "filled the pulpit" on Sunday mornings, and they recall as well Eva Ludgate, an evangelist of note during the World War I era.

Eva Ludgate had been surrounded all her life by women preachers. When her family joined College Church in 1908, they brought to the membership the colorful and fearless approach to evangelism associated with those who pioneered the Salvation Army.

The Ludgates had a lifetime of rich and varied ministry experiences in Canada and the Northeast. In 1882, Joseph Cornelius Ludgate (known locally as J. C.) emigrated from England to Ontario where he and his friend Jack Addie planted the Salvation Army. The Canadian Army became an instant sensation. When Ludgate married Salvation Army Captain Nellie Ryerson (a Methodist pastor's daughter) in 1884, a thousand people paid the Salvation Army's ten-cent entry fee to attend the two-hour "Hallelujah Wedding" at Belleville, Ontario's Bridge Street Methodist Church. (The local paper reported that four thousand more spectators lined the route to the reception at Belleville's City Hall.)

The Ludgates rose through the officer ranks in the Army: J. C. became a Brigadier. Eva Ludgate, their first child, grew up in a home where a passion for souls was first priority in their lives. The family worked first in Canada, then in New York under Evangeline Booth. Like other Army pioneers, the Ludgates used music and drama to draw crowds. J. C. played a concertina, and during his Army days the *New York Times* described him as "the long distance singer" for his popular hymn sings–a set program of fifty-one familiar hymns in sixty minutes–complete with an impromptu band, hand clapping, and handkerchief waving. In 1898, J. C. Ludgate set words to a Stephen Foster melody to create a popular gospel song, "Friendship with Jesus." The Ludgates brought creative energy and sturdy faith to their new connections in Wheaton.

Eva Ludgate took a more traditional route to ministry than her parents. After completing college and seminary, Eva was ordained at the Congregational Church of Burlington, Iowa, and installed as pastor of the Congregational Church in Danville, Iowa (1913). A few years later, she began devoting her time to evangelistic work. Ludgate filled the pulpit at College Church one Sunday morning in 1916 and three Sundays in August 1917 and preached as well at a union evening service on the high school lawn in Wheaton.

In 1917, the National Federation of Churches sent Ludgate to France to preach to American troops, and on her return she became president of the International Prayer Battalion, a women's organization committed to praying for military personnel. She died after an evangelistic campaign in the Philadelphia suburbs in December 1925 from a lingering injury sustained in a railroad accident. Charles Blanchard was literally penning the final words of her funeral sermon when he passed away on December 21, 1925.

In 1901, Congregational women began participating in the newly popular deaconess movement through which Protestant women received training for outreach among the urban poor. Under the auspices of particular congregations, deaconesses befriended the needy, cared for the sick, and did home visitation and evangelistic work in rough urban neighborhoods. The Congregational Deaconess Association was located in Chicago where the denomination established a training home in 1901. In 1904, Emily Muckridge, financial secretary of the Congregational Deaconess Association, presented the association's work to the CCC midweek service.

At the time, CCC had no deaconesses. The deaconess movement helped revive general Protestant interest in women's benevolent work within and through congregations. In 1917, an amendment to the Church Manual added two deaconesses as officers of College Church (making the officers the pastor, six elders, six deacons, two deaconesses, clerk, treasurer, head usher, and Sunday school superintendent).

CCC youth were organized into a Christian Endeavor Society. In the 1880s, congregation-based youth groups were an innovation, and Christian Endeavor was a Congregationalist venture from the start. Francis Clark organized the first Endeavor in Portland, Maine, in 1881 with the purpose of promoting "an earnest Christian life," increasing the "mutual acquaintanceship" of members, and making them "more useful in the service of God." The movement spread rapidly: by 1905 it had international branches and thousands of national chapters. Its pledge, literature, hymnals, and conventions mobilized thousands of young Protestants and gave youth work its own place in congregational life.

Protestant Associations

Beyond its denominational connections, CCC participated as well
in the broad network of associations through which American
Protestants historically channeled their energies. Congregationalists
featured prominently in organizing the great national enterprises
intended to promote American Christianity: the American Bible
Society, the American Tract Society, the American Sunday School
Union. They also helped local branches of these societies flourish, working under their banners as missionaries and colporteurs.
For example, in 1893, Minnie Worrell Blachly, daughter of an
Illinois Congregational pastor and a member of CCC, married
an American Bible Society missionary to Mexico, where in 1894
she found her own niche as president of the Mexican WCTU. In
the summer of 1893, church members traveled nationally among
Congregational churches to preach in the interests of the college and the National Christian Association while others undertook Sunday school missionary work in Nebraska, Michigan, and
the Dakotas. Locally, CCC funds and people cooperated in the
DuPage Sunday School Union's extension Sunday schools in
unchurched and rural areas.

Protestant impulses

Between 1865 and 1914, American Protestants found reasons for
concern as well as confidence about the future. Concern arose
from both intellectual and social realities: perceived conflicts
between science and faith as well as biblical criticism nurtured
doubts about the historic claims of Christianity at the same time
that massive immigration, industrialization, and urbanization
raised unprecedented ministry challenges. Confidence derived
from revivals, vigorous new youth movements, new approaches
to ministry training, and a growing interest in spreading the gospel. Missionary statesman Arthur T. Pierson called these hopeful

signs "forward movements," and he found many promising indicators in the late nineteenth century.

Energetic renewal movements invited Protestants to experience for themselves the faith they professed. Holiness ministries challenged people to be sanctified. The Keswick Movement promoted the "overcoming life." A fresh look at Hebrews 13:8–"Jesus Christ the same yesterday, and to day, and for ever"–cultivated interest in divine healing. Consideration of world events in the light of Scripture reinvigorated the conviction that the end times had come. Interest in these and related topics drew people from many denominations and thrived around publications, camp meetings, and evangelists. Overlapping networks sustained and spread interest at the grassroots, and some of them touched CCC through their influence on prominent members, their reach into the college, or coverage in the religious press. Much of the energy of late nineteenth-century revivalistic Protestantism radiated from D. L. Moody.

D. L. Moody and Emma Dryer

College Church members were aware of the Chicago congregation Moody had founded and sent it occasional support. In 1883, ties to the church strengthened when Charles Blanchard accepted appointment as pulpit supply at the Chicago Avenue Church (later Moody Memorial Church)–a surprising move for a new college president who had recently relinquished the CCC pulpit and who had deep scruples about Sunday commuting. For eighteen months, Blanchard took a Friday afternoon train to Chicago and, honoring his family's Sabbath-keeping principles, returned to Wheaton early on Monday morning. He devoted Saturdays and Sundays to the flourishing ministries at the Chicago Avenue Church, where he taught the Union Sunday school lesson to 800–900 teachers from Chicago congregations on Saturday afternoons and preached twice on Sundays.

Jonathan Blanchard, meanwhile, had often regretted in the *Cynosure* that Moody accepted support from lodge members, but a visit to Moody's summer Christian Worker's Conference in Northfield, Massachusetts, impressed Jonathan Blanchard with the potential of Moody's endeavors. In countless ways, the unordained Moody united Protestants around common objectives, facilitated new outreaches, and mobilized young Christians for gospel work. Moody had a hand in the success of the YMCA, Christian Endeavor, the Student Volunteer Movement, rescue missions, temperance work, revival efforts, Christian education, and a long list of other Protestant forward movements of the day.

At the Chicago Avenue Church, Charles Blanchard worked alongside the formidable Emma Dryer, an educator Moody had enlisted years earlier to engage in evangelistic work in the inner city. Dryer left an influential post as head of the female faculty at Illinois State Normal University to move to Chicago and train women for evangelistic work. She and Moody discussed preliminary plans for a Bible institute open to women and men, and she did all she could to lay a foundation while she waited for Moody to proceed. Moody's 1873–1875 revival services in Britain established him as the era's premier evangelist. On his return home, he settled his family in his Massachusetts hometown of Northfield rather than in Chicago (where the family home had been destroyed in the Chicago Fire), and his earlier plans for Chicago languished.

Dryer taught a large Bible class at the Chicago Avenue Church and enlisted Charles Blanchard's assistance in drawing Moody's attention back to a Bible institute in Chicago. Blanchard provided $500 and brought the well-known Bible teacher William G. Moorehead of Xenia Theological Seminary (Ohio) to run a short Christian worker's training course at the church. It attracted fifty young men and women. Similar events in 1884 and 1885 drew larger enrollments and amply demonstrated the potential for an institute. Moody agreed to proceed, and the Chicago Evangelization Society (later Moody Bible Institute) was established in 1886.

Dryer and others associated with the Bible institute found a warm welcome at Wheaton College and at College Church. A sense of partnership with Moody's Chicago-based outreaches thrived, especially after the Institute opened and again in cooperative evangelistic endeavors during the Columbian Exposition in 1893. Before long, Institute faculty settled in Wheaton. For a few years beginning in 1906, the popular British-born Bible teacher William Evans (a member of Moody Bible Institute's first graduating class in 1892) attempted to combine pastoral duties at CCC with teaching at Moody Bible Institute, but despite help from CCC's first (and temporary) assistant pastor, he found the task impossible. (The Evans family eventually relocated to California where William Evans taught at the Bible Institute of Los Angeles. His son, Louis Evans, became pastor of Hollywood Presbyterian Church; Louis Evans Jr. was Ronald Reagan's pastor at Bel Air Presbyterian Church.)

College Church experienced D. L. Moody's influence in indirect ways too. Moody helped popularize British evangelical authors and speakers. His endorsements assured the popularity of the writings of Charles Spurgeon, F. B. Meyer, and Horatius Bonar, as well as of his American friends A. J. Gordon, A. T. Pierson, and R. A. Torrey. Moody's song leader, Ira Sankey, popularized a new style of sacred song that quickly gained popularity. The most influential of Sankey's several hymnals was *Gospel Hymns 1–6*, a collection of seven hundred songs that publishers dubbed "the most valuable musical property in the world." Gospel hymns featured singable tunes, made wide use of refrains, and laid emphasis on personal testimony: "What a wonderful change in my life has been wrought since Jesus came into my heart"; "I was sinking deep in sin, far from the peaceful shore"; "'Twas a glad day when Jesus found me, when his strong arms were thrown around me"; "A wonderful Savior is Jesus, my Lord, a wonderful Savior to me."

In 1883, the College Church Sunday school purchased its first gospel hymnals, and soon Sunday evening services featured gospel hymn sings, a practice in place until well after World War II. The Saturday afternoon Preparatory Lectures preceding Communion also became occasions for extended gospel singing and Bible memorization as well as for solemn admonitions and personal testimonies. In 1901, the congregation bought Sankey's *Church Hymns and Gospel Songs*, and in 1903 it added Evangelist R. A. Torrey's *World Renowned Hymns*, 214 selections that combined familiar classics with what Torrey called "masterpieces of modern hymnology which appeared in connection with Mr. Moody's campaigns."

The Popularity of Premillennialism

Moody's matter-of-fact embrace of premillennialism helped popularize the view that Jesus would soon return. Premillennialists believed that the Second Coming might occur at any moment and was always imminent. It alone could put in motion the events that would make the world right: the world would never improve until Jesus returned to judge sin and set up his Kingdom. Postmillennialists who thought that preaching the gospel and reforming society would inaugurate the Kingdom of God were misguided. The men and women who embraced premillennialism testified that their immediate concerns changed: once they apprehended the imminence of Christ's return, they prioritized personal holiness (being ready for Christ's return) and evangelism (saving the souls of others from imminent doom). While

Jonathan Blanchard never clearly endorsed this view, he did not oppose it, and Charles Blanchard embraced it. Premillennialists pored over biblical prophecy and understood contemporary events as "signs of the times," harbingers of Christ's return. During the 1890s, Cyrus I. Scofield prepared detailed notes that explained the present unfolding of God's plan for the ages. In 1909 his notes, appended to the King James Version of the Bible, were published as the *Scofield Reference Bible.*

Premillennialist beliefs sometimes limited expectations about the value of thoroughgoing social reform. Not all College Church members changed their views on the end times, and the testimonies remained in place, but they easily became markers for personal behavior rather than objectives for national renewal in the march toward God's dawning Kingdom. "True" Christians kept the Sabbath; they neither drank nor danced nor gambled. Apart from its original context, the comprehensive Wesleyan social vision easily morphed into legalism.

A. B. Simpson and the CMA

Contemporary interest in divine healing also found an audience at CCC. The evangelist Jennie Smith brought to the college chapel her dramatic testimony of miraculous recovery after sixteen bedridden years. Her experience drew her into a larger network of people eager to experience all that God had for them. The contemporary growth of Christian Science aroused among evangelicals a curiosity about what the Bible said about the healing power of Christ; spiritualist "demonstrations" prompted interest in biblical supernaturalism; and the contemporary holiness movement, with its view of the indwelling empowering presence of the Holy Spirit, supported the belief that Christ "quickened the mortal body" physically as well as spiritually. Those who desired healing were encouraged by testimonies to healings in the popular religious press—popular books and articles on the subject by Carrie Judd Montgomery, A. J. Gordon, Charles Cullis, and Christian and Missionary Alliance founder A. B. Simpson—and "faith homes" where hospitality, Bible teaching, and "the prayer of faith" were propounded.

College Church people had direct personal connections to A. B. Simpson and the Christian and Missionary Alliance. A Canadian Presbyterian, Simpson had resigned a Manhattan pulpit to found a "gospel tabernacle" where seats were free and everyone was welcome. He mobilized people interested in Christ-centered piety into a network of small nondenominational groups known as the Christian Alliance. He promoted foreign missions through the International Missionary Alliance and the Missionary Training Institute (now Nyack College in Nyack, New York). In 1897, the merger of the two alliances created the Christian and Missionary Alliance (CMA). Simpson testified to healing from heart problems and developed a message he called the fourfold gospel: Christ the Savior, Healer, Sanctifier, and Coming King. In the first decades of the twentieth century, the CMA gradually became a denomination.

In the early twentieth century, CCC included people influenced by the Christian and Missionary Alliance, among them the Rev. W. H. Chandler and Charles Blanchard. Blanchard knew A. B. Simpson and attended and addressed several Alliance conventions. He stayed frequently at the Alliance headquarters in New York. His friend, J. C. Crawford of the Boone (Iowa) Biblical Institute, was a regional CMA leader. Wheaton College hosted annual CMA conventions during which Alliance leaders preached CCC Sunday services.

In 1912, CMA missionaries to China Mr. and Mrs. Philip Hinkey held special services. In 1916, CMA missionary widow Helen Galbraith Ekvall and her children joined CCC. In January 1917, she filled the pulpit on a Sunday morning and evening.

Helen Galbraith and her sister, Anna, had been pioneer Alliance missionaries to China. There in 1897 Helen married David Ekvall, another pioneer in north China, and there their children, Robert and Alice, were born. Robert Ekvall later became a noted CMA missionary in China and Tibet supported by CCC. In such ways, Alliance piety and priorities touched CCC.

The presence in Wheaton of a group of Free Methodists, meanwhile, provided opportunity for guidance on yielding to religious emotions. While commending the basic call to holiness, CCC leaders cautioned against excessive emotionalism. They strove for balance while recognizing the fluidity of evangelical Christianity. Before 1900, the boundaries of evangelicalism were still nebulous: "evangelical" commonly described the vast majority of American Protestants. A generation later, many found it necessary to clarify the movement's margins. But at the turn of the century, College Church participated in a richly textured evangelical stream that coursed through mainline denominations and independent movements alike.

In CCC, the confluence of mainline interests and revivalist piety produced a congregation engaged in missions, serious about spiritual nurture, committed to higher education, open to considerable participation by women, and involved in community affairs.

CHAPTER 3

CONFLICTS

The Church shall never perish!
Her dear Lord to defend,
To guide, sustain, and cherish
Is with her to the end.
Though there be those that hate her
And false sons in her pale,
Against both foe or traitor
She ever shall prevail.

SAMUEL J. STONE, 1866

IN AUGUST 1910, Charles Blanchard and his third wife, Frances Carothers, attended the eighteenth International Peace Conference in Stockholm as delegates of the Chicago branch of the American Peace Society, a pacifist organization established in 1828. The peace movement prospered as one of the Protestant crusades for a Christian America. Blanchard family participation reached back almost to the American Society's beginnings, and over the years, more societies arose to promote the cause. In February 1914, a $2 million donation from Andrew Carnegie inaugurated the Church Peace Union, an ecumenical venture dedicated to enlisting America's religious people to promote peace by eliminating specific forms of injustice.

A few months later, world events put the peace movement on hold. Archduke Ferdinand of Austria and his wife were assassinated in June 1914; in August the outbreak of World War I forced the cancellation of the International Peace Conference in

Vienna. In the United States, peace activists rallied to President Woodrow Wilson's rhetoric of neutrality while millions of other Protestants echoed former president Theodore Roosevelt's demand for American entry into the European war.

From 1860, the Blanchards and other New England Congregationalist members presented College Church and Wheaton College with the American Peace Society's case for nonbelligerency. But members of the church and college communities were free to differ, and in 1917 they united behind Wilson's call to arms.

For more than a decade after 1917, College Church faced different kinds of battles: first came the physical battles of the war in which the congregation lost two young men and sent three ordained men to minister to the troops; then came the theological battles known as the Fundamentalist-Modernist Controversy; finally, an internal debate split the church around the question of how to be faithful to conservative principles, rather than what to believe.

World War I

At noon on a spring morning in 1919, an impromptu parade led by Wheaton College faculty marched from the school to the Wheaton train station. Just an hour earlier, a telegram delivered to the college had announced the imminent arrival of the wounded navy lieutenant Charles Wayland Brooks on the 11:56 train. A decorated local boy who had studied at Wheaton Academy, Brooks was the son of much-loved former College Church pastor Jonas G. Brooks and was stopping at home en route to a rehabilitation center. Flags, trumpets, and singing gave the station a festive air, and the marchers followed the Brooks's car home and lingered long on the family's lawn just south of the college campus.

Brooks was one of ninety Wheaton College men and women

on active duty in the Great War. The vast majority had attended College Church during their student days; they were well-known to many in the congregation. As the war effort geared up, more than 135 men from the town of Wheaton answered their country's call. Their send-offs blended patriotism and faith as bands marched, pastors prayed, and civic leaders summoned everyone to find a way to help the cause. From war bonds to knitting circles to victory gardens, people across America did their part, and in towns like Wheaton, churches orchestrated much of the grassroots mobilization. Frequent union meetings at Wheaton's larger churches coordinated fund drives, recruited volunteers, and presented patriotic speakers.

Wheaton College and the town were proud of Charles Brooks and others like him, and the community mourned together as the list of local casualties gradually grew to twelve during the closing weeks of fighting. Toward the end of September 1918, the name of Russell Brooks, a marine aviator and Charles's brother, appeared on that list, which made Charles's homecoming more poignant than most. The boys' father, Rev. Jonas G. Brooks, meanwhile, was still in France where YMCA responsibilities kept him until the troops finally came home. Like the vast majority of American Protestants, the Brooks family seamlessly blended patriotism and faith. Russell and Charles Brooks enlisted in the navy in May 1917, a few weeks after their father, then College Church's pastor, preached a sermon entitled "Shall We Enlist? Who Is Patriotic?"

Wartime pastor, Jonas G. Brooks

College Church people knew Jonas (J. G.) Brooks well when they called him to the pulpit in the spring of 1910. An 1893 graduate of Wheaton College and a full-time evangelist for the Illinois Congregational Association, Brooks often made the pages of *The Advance*, the weekly Congregationalist paper. Enthusiastic reports documented the results that followed his preaching—members added or reclaimed, churches organized, coffers filled. In 1906, for example, Brooks's meetings in the village of De Pue, Illinois, raised $900 to support a regular pastor for the town's Congregational church and added fifty members to that body.

During his first five years at College Church, such indicators of spiritual health continued to follow his ministry. Brooks welcomed 154 new members for a net gain of 83, or 26 percent growth. Increased giving enabled expanded benevolences. Just eight months after Brooks arrived, *The Advance* commended College Church's generosity: the congregation had increased its giving to seven Congregational societies, outfitted two missionaries for India (the "outfits" included a pump organ for one and a typewriter for the other), contributed to the support of ten specific missionaries, and paid the full salary of the Rev. W. C. Cooper, missionary to Turkey. Attendance trended upward.

Under the direction of the Rev. Hugh Cork, secretary of the International Sunday School Association, the College Church Sunday school thrived. It met at noon, following the 10:30 morning service. Sunday evening services were at 7:00 p.m., with the Christian Endeavor Society meeting at 6:00 p.m. Student prayer meetings on Tuesday evenings and church prayer meetings on Wednesdays at 7:45 p.m. rounded out the regular schedule. The church pressed toward its goal: "Every church member in the Sunday school; every Sunday school member in the church." Sunday school class socials, open houses, cottage meetings, the annual church New Year's Day dinner, and college events, meanwhile, nurtured a sense of community.

The busy congregational schedule did not diminish Brooks's attention to public matters. While he was pastor of College Church, he ran for Congress in 1910 and 1912, and for the Illinois State Assembly in 1914, each time on the Prohibition ticket.

Brooks led College Church in tumultuous times for the nation. American relations with Germany deteriorated quickly after 1914, especially after Germany violated Belgian neutrality and sank the UK's RMS *Lusitania* in 1915. A rush of Allied propaganda flooded the nation. Three staunch Protestant leaders with national profiles proposed different courses of action: Theodore Roosevelt demanded war, President Wilson urged neutrality, and William Jennings Bryan yearned for peace. Charles Blanchard exchanged several letters with President Wilson in which both expressed the desire for peace while admitting the likelihood of war.

As a peace activist, Charles Blanchard dreaded the effects of a spirit of war on the culture, but in 1917, Wilson reluctantly asked Congress for a declaration of war. The president framed the war as a holy cause: "The right is more precious than peace, and we shall fight . . . for a universal dominion of right by such a concert of free peoples as shall bring peace and safety to all nations." Blanchard became convinced that Wilson followed solid moral principles that Christians must obey. A devout Presbyterian and the son of a Southern Presbyterian pastor, Wilson freely used the familiar language of the King James Version to justify his policies and mobilize the nation. On Good Friday, April 6, 1917, Congress declared war, and American Protestants largely fell into line in support of a "war to end all wars" and a vision for a future peace based on democratic ideals.

The key role of the YMCA in the military

In the absence of military chaplains, the YMCA and, to a lesser extent, the Salvation Army took much of the responsibility for meeting the spiritual and social needs of the troops at home and abroad. Under the guidance of 200 prominent Americans constituted into the YMCA War Work Council, YMCA-paid staff swelled to 26,000, and 35,000 volunteers augmented the ranks. In France, YMCA Rest and Recreation Centers eventually accommodated nearly 2 million American troops. YMCA and Salvation Army chaplains conducted religious services in some 4,000 YMCA huts and tents set up in every camp at home and abroad. YMCA canteens and post exchanges operated in France under army regulations, and the YMCA provided humanitarian services to over 5 million prisoners of war.

When the United States entered the war, College Church, Wheaton College, and the Wheaton community already had long associations with the YMCA. A chapter of the collegiate YMCA existed on campus in close relationship to the local chapter of the Student Volunteer Movement for Foreign Missions. In May 1917, a YMCA traveling secretary addressed a union meeting at Wheaton's Methodist Church to raise money for work among the troops. Soon YMCA efforts claimed more from College Church than money. College Church Sunday school superintendent Hugh Cork volunteered for YMCA religious work and was posted to a camp in Wisconsin.

Impressed with the enormous need and opportunity, Cork urged his friends to consider similar work. Pastor Brooks visited Cork at Camp Robinson in Sparta, Wisconsin, where 6,000 men were in basic training, and late in 1917, after repeated trips for camp ministry, he resigned the pastorate of College Church to take charge of YMCA religious work at Camp Robinson. Early in 1918, he was posted to France as a chaplain to the American Expeditionary Force. In Wheaton as elsewhere, church support for the war effort was strong. College Church released Pastor Brooks with reluctance, but with enthusiasm for his new work. The College Church choir director and other young men were drafted. Hugh Cork, meanwhile, rose quickly through YMCA ranks to become director of religious work in the South for the army YMCA. Rev. J. C. Ludgate became YMCA chaplain at Kelly Field, the premier training base for aviators near San Antonio, Texas.

Preachers in Wheaton and across the nation urged their congregations to purchase war bonds, conserve resources, and supply the troops, and the enthusiastic response made rationing unnecessary. While historic peace churches like the Mennonites and the Society of Friends and a few Social Gospelers stood apart, most Protestants showed their patriotism by getting involved. Contributions enabled Bible societies to supply Bibles and religious literature to the troops. Theodore Roosevelt prepared a message for the troops that deftly blended biblical morality and American values, and it was inserted into the free New Testaments distributed to each soldier. The weekly Wheaton newspaper devoted part of its front page to letters from local soldiers and listed all draftees under the heading "Roll of Honor." In bold type at the end of the Roll were the names of those who died. By the end of the war, two were from College Church, each the son of a YMCA chaplain–Willis Cork and Russell Brooks.

YMCA work with the American Expeditionary Force offered Pastor J. G. Brooks a challenge suited to his abilities. He had served College Church for over seven years, but he was an evangelist at heart. After nearly a year in two huge army camps at the front in France, Brooks was assigned to special work among the 110,000 black soldiers scattered among many camps in France. When the troops returned, Brooks remained with the YMCA until 1921 when he accepted a call to the Congregational Church in Payson, Illinois.

During his years of domestic YMCA work, Brooks traveled widely to encourage YMCA evangelism. The YMCA's magazine, *Young Men*, reported in February 1919 under the heading "Live Religious Work" that Brooks's visit to Elgin, Illinois, brought to that association's religious work "a new impulse of effort." His "addresses on prayer, personal work, the deeper Christian life, and his sane evangelistic messages, have vitalized the Associations he has visited." The Brooks family lived in Wheaton during J. G. Brooks's travels, and Lillian Brooks took a prominent place in the Women's Missionary Society at College Church. J. G. Brooks remained a trustee of Wheaton College after the family moved to Payson. By the late 1920s, they were back in Wheaton.

In 1936, Brooks's son Charles Wayland Brooks ran for governor of Illinois on the Republican ticket but lost to the Democrat incumbent. In 1940, Charles narrowly won election as United States Republican senator from Illinois, an office he held through 1948.

World War I not only took young men and women away: it also forced missionaries to return home, and they helped supply the pulpit in the absence of a pastor. College Church heard frequent firsthand reports of atrocities in Turkey as the Ottoman Empire collapsed. When they were in the area, J. G. Brooks or Hugh Cork preached. The pulpit was also supplied by Moody Bible Institute faculty, various evangelists from the congregation (including Henry Stough, whose energetic wife, Helen, was elected the church's first female Sunday school superintendent), and friends from the Congregational Association.

Pastors Franklin Neitz and John Welsh

In October 1918, the influenza epidemic reached Wheaton, and health officials closed area churches for several weeks. When College Church gathered again on November 3, a new pastor, Rev. Franklin C. Neitz, was in place. Neitz was reared in the Evangelical Association, a group that united several small German revivalist groups. He had attended his denomination's college, Northwestern (now North Central) College in Naperville, and graduated in the class of 1888. As a student, he signed the Student Volunteer Movement pledge indicating his commitment to missionary service, and in 1890 he and his wife sailed under the Evangelical Association for Tokyo. Just two years later, she succumbed to smallpox. Neitz returned home with his young children and received Congregational ordination. He came to Wheaton from a pastorate in St. Charles and remained until May 1921, when the family moved to California.

In August 1921, the congregation called John Welsh, pastor of First Congregational Church in Elgin, as pastor for a one-year term. The church renewed his contract annually until Welsh resigned in 1926. Before coming to College Church, Welsh had led several strong northern Illinois churches and spent two years as evangelist Billy Sunday's front man, arranging Sunday's national schedule.

College Church and Fundamentalism

Already before Welsh arrived, College Church and Wheaton College began identifying regularly with people and associations connected to the emerging network of fundamentalists. In the nineteenth century, the vast majority of Protestants were evangelicals, and that label required little elaboration: it described Bible-believing, Christ-honoring, gospel-driven people in every major denomination. Toward the end of the century, however, modern biblical scholarship and science challenged the authority of the Bible and questioned traditional understandings of Christian faith. Several well-publicized denominational heresy trials drew battle lines but failed to stem the tide of change.

In 1878, participants in an annual nondenominational Bible conference (known as Believers' Meeting for Bible Study) convened by Presbyterian pastor James H. Brookes summarized "true Christianity" in a fourteen-point statement of faith. In 1910,

Presbyterians identified five points the denomination considered faithful Christians must hold: the Virgin Birth, the substitutionary Atonement, the physical Resurrection, the authenticity of biblical miracles, and the inspiration of Scripture. Between 1910 and 1915, every pastor, Sunday school superintendent, and missionary of every Protestant denomination received free copies of twelve modestly sized publications collectively called *The Fundamentals: A Testimony to the Truth*. Funded by oil magnate Lyman Stewart, the books presented ninety essays on subjects the editors considered essential to Christian orthodoxy. More expansive than the Presbyterian "five points," *The Fundamentals* were edited by Amzi Clarence (A. C.) Dixon and R. A. Torrey, both former pastors of the Moody Church and well-known to members of College Church.

In the first decade of the twentieth century, it was not always easy to know who was who, and these lists attempted clarifications. The long tradition of cooperation grounded in common devotion to Christ, the pressing task of world missions, the claims of the urban poor, and voluntary associations like the YMCA and the American Bible Society featured Christ-centered piety and devotion and easily masked profound theological differences. Conservatives themselves divided in their responses to new movements within their own ranks like Pentecostalism or holiness associations.

The situation was further complicated by the institutional realities of American Protestantism: most people had ties to both denominations and voluntary associations. In some of these, theological differences mattered more than in others, and new theological visions tended to spawn new voluntary societies. As academic debates about the Bible filtered down into the churches, questions arose: should conservatives withdraw and form "pure" agencies? Or should they hold steady in the associations to which they belonged on the assumption that truth would prevail?

Cooperation around the war effort postponed a crisis (although YMCA chaplains represented a wide spectrum of Protestant opinions), but as the Great War came to an end and the nation debated the terms of peace, vocal Northern conservatives led by a handful of forceful pulpit orators banded together in the World's Christian Fundamentals Association. The impetus came from William Bell Riley, a longtime friend of Charles Blanchard and a trustee of Wheaton College. Editor of *The Christian Fundamentalist* since 1891 and pastor of First Baptist Church in Minneapolis, Riley convened a conference in Philadelphia in 1919 at which an organization took shape. Charles Blanchard helped draft its "Statement of Faith," a document that harmonized for the most part with the earlier lists. But unlike the five major points of Presbyterian belief, this document affirmed the premillennial return of Christ.

In 1929, College Church decided to add the Statement of Faith of the World's Christian Fundamentals Association (known as the Philadelphia Creed) to its Manual, keeping it separate from the Articles of Faith members had affirmed since 1860, but presenting it as a statement endorsed by the congregation. Placed side by side, the Articles of Faith and the so-called Philadelphia Statement illustrate the changed theological climate. Adjectives had been added to give precision to the general affirmations that once sufficed: fundamentalists affirmed the *Virgin* Birth, the *substitutionary* Atonement, the *physical* Resurrection, the *premillennial* return of Christ.

Strong personalities on both sides of the debate

As College Church moved toward expecting more precise doctrinal unanimity, Northern Baptists and Presbyterians were mired in very public controversies that swirled around personalities as well as beliefs. Denominational quarrels made the headlines in the nation's largest newspapers, thanks, in part, to the prominence of people on both sides of the debate. One of the nation's ablest pulpiteers, Harry Emerson Fosdick, a Baptist, had an unusual appointment as preaching pastor at New York City's historic First Presbyterian Church. In 1922 he delivered a sermon titled "Shall the Fundamentalists Win?" Fosdick accused fundamentalists of "drawing a deadline of doctrine around the church" that left no room for differences of opinion and denied the name "Christian" to any who could not agree with the most conservative assertions. The sermon was widely publicized, and Fosdick resigned rather than become a target in the surging Presbyterian fray.

At Princeton Seminary, meanwhile, J. Gresham Machen, the distinguished professor of New Testament, issued a scathing denunciation of liberal Christianity in a small book whose title succinctly summarized its thesis: *Christianity and Liberalism.* For Machen, the two were polar opposites. The religious press followed the growing acrimony within denominations, and new periodicals idealized or castigated the principal actors. In June 1936, the Northern Presbyterian General Assembly defrocked Machen. College Church members followed the well-publicized trials and appeals, and a growing number of conservative partisans made their case at the church and college.

Long associations with Moody Bible Institute as well as recent participation in fundamentalist conventions made wide exposure to fundamentalist speakers logical, but not everyone at College Church endorsed the separatism and angry denunciations that came to be fundamentalist hallmarks. When someone proposed during a church business meeting that the church endorse *The Fundamentals,* another church member promptly moved that members vote on them one by one. The result? No action. Participation in the Congregational Association moderated harsh fundamentalist attitudes too. The denomination helped keep broad commitments and purposes in view, and its decentralized polity enabled Congregationalists to avoid their own denominational schism.

A New Church Building on the College Campus

In 1922, members of College Church began to discuss seriously the need for a dedicated church home. For more than sixty years, they had worshiped in the main building of Wheaton College surrounded by classrooms and faculty offices. Membership now hovered around four hundred, and leaders recognized an acute need for accessible space as well as dedicated Sunday school rooms, a fully equipped kitchen, and church parlors. Accessibility was a serious concern. The college building perched atop a hill, and the sanctuary occupied much of its third floor: getting there taxed the strength of aging and infirm members. Discussions about installing an elevator failed to make headway. The congregation now imagined a larger chapel with adjustable partitions that could be removed to expand seating.

In this discussion, no one proposed leaving the college campus; the church's identification with the college should be a lasting one, they concurred, and that was best accomplished by staying on-site. They did not want to give the impression that the church had separated from the college on matters of doctrine or practice. So they approached college trustees with a proposal to build in partnership with the college on the northwest corner of the campus.

The overlapping leadership of church and college simplified the process of a joint venture. College Church's pastor, John Welsh, was a Wheaton College trustee. The college and church both appointed committees of three to oversee the project, and both raised funds that they agreed to disburse through the college. All donations from resident church members were reckoned as church contributions, while the college constituency beyond the church had its own fund-raising initiative. The proposed building would be primarily a church, but it would accommodate large college events–a joint committee of operation would control the allocation of space. Building maintenance would be calculated on the basis of use, with the church footing the full bill when the college was not in session. The final agreement included a process for terminating the arrangement: either party might do so in writing with two years' notice. Termination required payment by the college of a fair allowance for the current value of the congregation's total investment, the allowance to be determined by three appraisals.

With the agreement signed, both groups turned to fundraising. Church members reduced costs by volunteering labor. On Labor Day in 1924, for example, two hundred members turned out at 7:00 a.m. to help with the excavation, saving the project at least $600; horses and motorized equipment worked side by side attesting to the changing times. The women served coffee, lemonade, and lunch, and the day ended with the reading of a local poet's ode for the new chapel. At least, that was the formal schedule. For some church children, however, the day began long before sunrise. Their teacher, elder D. A. Straw, had challenged them to be the first to break ground. Two boys dug a hole at 3:45 a.m., but the prize went to thirteen-year-old Esther Brooks, daughter of former pastor J. G. Brooks, who arrived on site with her wheelbarrow and shovel at 3:00 a.m. On Thanksgiving Day a large group gathered for the laying of the cornerstone. It read: "Wheaton College Church and Chapel, erected A.D. 1924 for Christ and His Kingdom." (The building would later be named Pierce Chapel.)

Construction proceeded apace, and enthusiasm for present and future ministries ran high. The talented musician Wendell P. Loveless, soon to be a fixture on Moody radio, was College Church chorister, and a new hymnal, *Tabernacle Hymns No. 2*, edited by evangelist Paul Rader and composer George C. Stebbins, provided a mix of familiar hymns and newer gospel songs. The Sunday school, average attendance two hundred, moved its meeting from noon to 9:00 a.m. Socials for teenagers, a dinner for fund-raisers, and ministries including jail services and mission Sunday schools filled the calendar. More than three hundred people attended the annual College Church New Year's Day dinner in 1925, held as usual in the Ladies Building (now Williston Hall). Early in 1925, church families selected their pews, anticipating the completion of the new building in time for the college's 1925 commencement exercises (unfortunately, this did not happen). Membership, including nonresidents, inched over 500 for the first time.

On Sunday morning, June 22, 1925, College Church welcomed J. Gresham Machen—then the nation's most distinguished conservative biblical scholar—to its pulpit. The Princeton Seminary professor chose as his topic "The Unseen Things." Peter Philpott, pastor of the Moody Church, gave that year's commencement address. The presence of these men in the College Church pulpit underscored the solidarity in the college and congregation with those who championed the general view that the "old-time religion" was adequate for the modern world. Philpott was a dispensationalist whose theology was summarized in the notes of the best-selling *Scofield Reference Bible*, while Machen looked to the Westminster Confession of Faith, subscribed to Princeton's famous stance on biblical inerrancy, and only separated from his denomination when it rejected him.

Just before the new sanctuary was finally ready for use in the fall of 1925, College Church members enjoyed a rare treat in their old sanctuary. Robert Harkness, the famous Australian accompanist for the worldwide evangelistic tours of Charles Alexander and R. A. Torrey, demonstrated his musical skills at the church. An author and composer of many hymn tunes, Harkness was famous for impromptu variations on any hymn tunes his audiences selected. His correspondence courses for piano set new standards for accompaniment styles for gospel singing.

A celebration and a farewell

College Church gathered for the first time in its new sanctuary for the wedding of two popular soon-to-be missionaries, Mary Park and Earl Winsor, on Thursday evening, November 5, 1925. The college used the space on November 9 to confer an honorary doctorate on Peter Philpott. On Wednesday, November 18, over a thousand people overflowed the sanctuary for the formal dedication services. Cream-colored woodwork, white walls, and large windows combined to brighten the interior, and the sounds of a new pipe organ filled the hall. The college faculty sat on the platform; Charles Blanchard, nearing the end of his forty-three-year presidency, prayed; the church choir sang the "Hallelujah Chorus" and Johann Sebastian Bach's setting of Martin Luther's "With grateful hearts we all are met."

Evangelist Henry Stough read the Scriptures, and William Bell Riley delivered the dedicatory sermon. Riley had emerged within the Northern Baptist Convention as a leader among the "fighting fundamentalists" who charged themselves with the task of exposing liberal views wherever they surfaced among American Protestants. A skilled orator and organizer, his dedicatory message developed a favorite fundamentalist theme–the future Kingdom of the Messiah. Basing his remarks on Micah 4, he spoke of the last days, the last war, and the last king.

The dedication of the new facility was one of Charles Blanchard's last public acts. A month later, the ailing president died: his funeral was the first one conducted in the new sanctuary. The church and college faced a new era. As the leading figures in both, Jonathan and Charles Blanchard had influenced the course of these institutions for sixty-five years. There was no obvious successor for the college presidency, and the board turned to one of its own, College Church pastor John Welsh, for interim leadership. On January 6, 1926, the church voted to lend its pastor to the college. Clergy and missionaries within the congregation– including former pastor J. G. Brooks–stepped up to serve the congregation in various ways, and church records report that visiting preachers and missionaries ministered "with deep spiritual power." One visitor in the pulpit was the famous British pastor, conference speaker, and author F. B. Meyer, then on his last tour of the United States. Another was J. Frank Norris, the acknowledged leader of fundamentalists in the South (and grandfather of long-time College Church member Lillian Smith).

J. Oliver Buswell, Third President of Wheaton College

Early in February 1926, J. Oliver Buswell, pastor of Grace Reformed Church in Brooklyn, conducted a week of special services at College Church and Wheaton College to which students responded by urging Buswell to remain another week. The Wheaton College *Record* described Buswell's ministry with adjectives like "firm, uncompromising, unemotional, rich." Buswell could not extend his February visit, but his popularity with students encouraged college trustees to pursue him as a candidate for president. On March 17, 1926, the trustees presented Buswell as the new president of Wheaton College. He assumed his duties on April 1.

Two months later, he introduced Lewis Sperry Chafer, founder of the Evangelical Theological College (later Dallas Theological Seminary), as Wheaton's commencement speaker and conferred on him an honorary doctorate. Chafer reciprocated in 1927 by awarding Buswell his school's first honorary doctorate. In September 1926, former acting president John

Welsh (who had hoped for the college presidency himself) resigned the College Church pastorate. Buswell, meanwhile, stepped easily into Blanchard's leadership role at the church as well as the college. He recommended friends who filled the pulpit for several months after John Welsh's departure.

In June 1927, the church called William R. Dodd to its pulpit. A 1905 graduate of Princeton Seminary, Dodd came to College Church from the Lafayette Avenue Presbyterian Church, a historic congregation in the heart of St. Louis. Like J. Oliver Buswell, he was a staunch ally of conservatives in the well-publicized quarrels then dividing the Presbyterian Church. Dodd's selection and Buswell's influence seemed likely to push College Church along a narrower path in its associations with other Protestants. By 1929, in his role as college president, Buswell solicited advice from a board of counselors that included such fundamentalist stalwarts as James M. Gray, William Bell Riley, A. Z. Conrad, and A. C. Gaebelein.

An influx of fundamentalism

One indicator of internal flux was the response to a motion on June 29, 1926, offered by Elsie Dow, longtime church leader and college professor, to proceed with the usual summer Sunday evening union services. Such motions had been little more than perfunctory over the years: College Church always took a leading role in the summer street preaching and outdoor services sponsored jointly by area churches. This time, though, the motion failed, and a special business meeting was called for July 6 to discuss the matter. The motion failed again, by a mere three votes. The Church Manual committed College Church members to a solidly conservative theology, but the vote on union services pointed toward emerging disagreements about fundamentalist separatism that grew more urgent as Buswell's influence widened.

Perceptive onlookers might have noticed another indicator of change in the Wheaton College *Bulletin* for 1928. Until then, college students were required to attend College Church unless they belonged to another denomination or filed a parental request. That requirement disappeared in 1928. Also, for the first time, the 1927 *Bulletin* included a college statement of faith: the 1919 Statement of the World's Christian Fundamentals Association.

Already in the fall of 1925, church members had discussed a motion to leave their denomination. Since the college attracted an interdenominational student body and many Methodist and Baptist students opted to attend College Church rather than churches of their denominations, College Church should become in fact what it already was in spirit—an independent interdenominational church. Fundamentalist impulses clearly motivated those who proposed this change: they referenced the influence of "the rapid development of the apostasy within the organized church so apparent not only at the home base but also in missionary enterprises here and overseas." They proposed the Moody Church or the Church of the Open Door (Los Angeles) as models. The motion failed, but its proponents did not give up.

Then, in March 1927, College Church members protested a ruling from the Illinois Congregational Association that forbade congregations to withdraw from the Association without the advice and approval of the Association. "We cannot be bound by the advice of any body," the church responded. "We believe in the principle of the independence of the local church. We cannot join in any action that limits it."

James Oliver Buswell easily became the leader of those who pointed the church in a more conservative direction. He came to Wheaton from a Dutch Reformed pastorate but was a Presbyterian by education and ordination. A premillennialist but not a dispensationalist, he was the son of a Presbyterian minister who took his theological training at McCormick Theological Seminary, and would later be awarded a doctorate from the University of Chicago.

His ardent sympathy for fundamentalist principles was evident long before he took a prominent role in the well-publicized Presbyterian schisms of the 1930s. As soon as Buswell arrived in Wheaton, College Church felt the influence of his convictions about the direction of American Christianity. A warm supporter of J. Gresham Machen, Buswell applauded Machen's decision to leave Princeton in 1929 to establish Westminster Theological Seminary as a conservative alternative to a reorganized Princeton Seminary.

Matters before the National Congregational Association played into the hands of those who thought the times demanded basic changes at College Church. The ecumenical impulse had blossomed in 1908 in the formation of the Federal Council of the Churches of Christ and during World War I in the work of the YMCA. This continued in the 1920s as mainline denominations took halting steps toward the creation of what later became the World Council of Churches. Advocates of ecumenism encouraged better communication and closer cooperation among denominations that shared the same roots. They did not push for organic union, but rather for federation.

The list of denominations related to Congregationalism included the Universalist Association. The mere mention of any form of cooperation with Universalists seemed to prove the point that fundamentalist separatists pressed—denominations were apostate, and true Christians had no choice but to withdraw. Congregational records do not substantiate serious consideration of a merger, but that hardly mattered. Perception was everything—after all, even if merger talks failed, fundamentalist separatists considered the ecumenical movement itself an ominous sign of the times.

The matter came before College Church. It amounted to a discussion about withdrawing from the Congregational Association. Those who urged leaving the denomination used the same arguments that members voted down in 1925. Talk of ties to Universalists merely added fuel to the long-smoldering fire. The other side preferred to hold steady, maintaining that abandoning other Bible-preaching, gospel-driven Congregational churches in the Association over a threat that had not materialized weakened the witness for truth in the denomination. Buswell insisted on circulating an invitation to local Congregational churches to a council to consider the denominational state of affairs and discuss forming a new fundamentalist Congregational association. Only five churches sent representatives, and none was willing to consider withdrawing from the Congregational Association.

A Church Split

The growing discontent within College Church came to a head in 1929. The June 21 edition of the weekly newspaper *Wheaton Illinoian* placed this headline front and center: "College Church Dissension Splits Congregation." The actual break had come with a vote on June 4 on whether or not to leave the Congregational Association. By a majority of three (the vote was 149-146), the members voted for College Church to remain affiliated. The disaffected minority (including President Buswell) withdrew, and on Sunday, June 16, two separate services, both on the college campus, accommodated the membership of the church. The College Church of Christ met as usual in the chapel, while the new "interdenominationalist faction" gathered in the old chapel in Blanchard Hall. Most of the members with ties to Moody Bible Institute went with the new group, and they led the services on that first Sunday. The Rev. Dodd, meanwhile, submitted his resignation. The local paper predicted correctly that "rifles will be cleared away amiably" but that reconciliation would not follow.

On June 28, 1929, the newly formed Wheaton College Interdenominational Church (soon renamed Wheaton Bible Church) ran its first ad in the local newspaper. It promised a full slate of services through the hot summer months–Sunday school at 10:00 a.m., morning and evening services, Christian Endeavor, and a midweek prayer and testimony meeting. A Women's Missionary Society was already in place. Christian educator and author Clarence Benson preached on the second Sunday morning, and E. J. Pace, cartoonist for the *Sunday School Times*, led the evening service. College Church lost its popular music director, Wendell P. Loveless, to the new congregation.

For a few weeks, the College Church of Christ submitted no announcements of services to the local paper. It resumed on July 19 with word that former pastor John Welsh would speak in the morning service on July 21 and the congregation would participate in a union service featuring the pastor of Trinity Episcopal Church in the evening. College Church members had voted soon after the split to resume union services: the choice showed that differences ran deeper than passing talk about Universalists.

On July 28, former pastor William Dodd preached for the Interdenominational Church. An expanded newspaper ad left no doubt about the congregation's fundamentalist purpose: "This fellowship stands firmly for the Faith of our Fathers. If you love the old Gospel and preaching of the Bible, come and join us." In September 1929, Wheaton College professor of history Herbert Moule became the acting pastor of The College Church of Christ. In 1930, the Rev. Arthur D. Penney of the First Presbyterian Church of Miami, Florida, accepted a temporary call to the College Church pulpit. Ill health had driven Penney from full-time ministry years earlier, and he became a Florida

Jonathan Blanchard, the first president of Wheaton College, was pastor of The Church of Christ in Wheaton from 1860 to 1862.

RIGHT: Freeborn Garretson Baker was a music professor at Wheaton College and the first music director at The Church of Christ in Wheaton. In 1868, he established the foundation for the church's choral music and congregational singing that continues to this day.

BELOW: The Church of Christ sanctuary on the third floor of Blanchard Hall at Wheaton College. The congregation worshiped there from 1872 to 1925.

ABOVE RIGHT: J. C. Webster was a distinguished clergyman, social activist, and Wheaton College professor whose disagreements with Jonathan Blanchard precipitated a church schism (1877–1878).

ABOVE LEFT: Elsie Storrs Dow came to The Church of Christ in 1877. A professor of English at Wheaton College for more than fifty years, she was an active church leader. Dow and her colleague Elder D. A. Straw began College Church's Sunday morning children's church.

Charles Blanchard and his third wife, Frances Carothers Blanchard. The second president of Wheaton College, Charles Blanchard was pastor of College Church from 1878 to 1883. "Mrs. President Blanchard," as his wife was known, was a strong leader whose opinion was often invited on church matters.

ABOVE LEFT: Ordained at College Church in 1882, George Filian was the first missionary formally commissioned by the congregation. An Armenian, he served first in the Ottoman (Turkish) Empire and then among Armenian immigrants in the United States.

ABOVE CENTER: Wheaton College's first international student, Anastasios Zaraphonites (class of 1873), was supported by College Church during his years in Greece as a medical missionary.

ABOVE RIGHT: William T. Osborne, a former slave, was a Wheaton College graduate and a member of College Church. An early graduate of the Wesleyan Theological Seminary (established in 1882) that met on the Wheaton College campus, Osborne became a pastor in the African Methodist Episcopal Church.

College Church Messenger

J. G. Brooks
Pastor in Wheaton

Our Church Home

W. C. Cooper
Pastor in Turkey

OUR AIM

Every Church Member In The Sunday School
Every Sunday School Member In The Church

OUR NINETEEN ELEVEN TEXT

Let no man seek his own, but every man another's wealth.—I. Cor. 10:24.

College Congregational Church

Wheaton, Illinois

Rev. J. G. Brooks, Pastor - - - - Phone 2642

.

"Come thou with us and we will do thee good."

49
32

OPPOSITE PAGE: During Jonas G. Brooks's pastorate from 1910 to 1917, College Church retained missionary W. C. Cooper as its pastor in Turkey, paying his full salary. Cooper played a significant role in relief efforts in the Balkans prior to World War I.

ABOVE LEFT: The Rev. Eva Ludgate, a Congregationalist pastor and evangelist, was a member of College Church along with her parents and siblings. She preached at College Church several times before undertaking evangelistic work among the troops in France in 1917.

ABOVE RIGHT: J. C. (Joseph Cornelius) Ludgate, Eva Ludgate's father, was a former Salvation Army officer who wrote gospel songs (the best known was "Friendship with Jesus"), supplied the pulpit, and led congregational singing with his concertina.

"𝕭uilding 𝕱or 𝕺ur 𝕸aster"

"At Home and Abroad"

⚔ ⚔ ⚔

"AS THOU DIDST SEND ME INTO THE WORLD,
EVEN SO SENT I THEM INTO THE WORLD."
— JOHN 17:18

JONAS G. BROOKS
Illinois State Evangelist

HUGH CORK
World S. S. Worker

GERTRUDE KELLOGG, F
Shansi Province, (N) Ch

JOSEPHINE KENNEDY, M. D.
Fukien Province, China

MORGAN TUCKER, Le
Chicago Boys Club

𝕿here 𝕬re 𝕸any 𝕭uilders in the world, builders of buildings, of books, of pictures, of businesses, but the greatest of all builders is the man builder. The business of man-making heads the list of all callings.

𝕺ur 𝕸ork is to hold up Christ, to keep Him in men's thoughts so that the Divine Spirit can get hold of the conscience to perform His great work of transforming the life. The highest of all obligations is the religious. Are you concerned?

𝕲od 𝕯oes 𝕹ot carry forward His work independently of human agency.

𝕿he 𝕮ollege 𝕮hurch of 𝕮hrist and 𝕸heaton 𝕮ollege are making a joint effort for better and greater things in the interest of the community and its student body. We earnestly seek your co-operation. Will you share the load?

𝕺ur 𝕻resent 𝕻roject, 𝕬 𝕹ew 𝕮hurch 𝕳ome and 𝕮hapel requires that we underwrite a Building Fund of $135,000. You can assist greatly in the progress of this good cause by contributing financially.

⚔ ⚔ ⚔

AMY A. WINSOR, Missionary
Belgian Congo, Africa

"GOD LOVETH A CHEERFUL GIVER."
— II COR. 9:7

LOUISE MEEBOLD, Missi
Central China

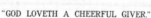

WHEATON COLLEGE
CHARLES A. BLANCHARD, *President*

COLLEGE CHURCH OF CHRIST
JOHN W. WELSH, *Pastor*

COLLEGE ALUMNI ASSOCIATION
JUDGE CHARLES D. CLARK, *President*
RALPH L. WHEATON, *Vice-President*   EARL A. WINSOR, *Secretary*
JUDGE FRANK E. HERRICK, *Vice-President*   JOHN WHITAKER, *Treasurer*
LIEUT. COL. H. L. KELLOGG, *Vice-President*

CHURCH FINANCE COMMITTEE
HOWARD IRWIN, *Chairman*
F. K. MANN   JAS. E. PHILLIPS
MRS. L. B. WOOD   MRS. H. R. STOUGH
WM. A. MCDONALD, *Treasurer*

JOS. M. WEAVER, *Treasurer Wheaton College*

Courtesy of College Church in Wheaton

Courtesy of the Wheaton College Archives

OPPOSITE PAGE: In the early 1920s, College Church and Wheaton College appealed jointly for funds to build a new sanctuary on campus. At that time, all Wheaton students were expected to attend College Church. This flyer pictures Wheaton graduates in full-time Christian ministries.

ABOVE: In 1924, two hundred College Church members of all ages spent Labor Day clearing the ground for the new sanctuary, saving the church $600. The women provided refreshments. Three children–Esther Brooks and James and Irving Phillips–dug the first holes before 4 a.m.

BELOW: The interior of the sanctuary on the west side of the college campus (now Pierce Chapel). The building was owned jointly by College Church and Wheaton College and opened in 1925.

ACROSS SPREAD: During the 1930s and '40s, College Church sponsored annual Victorious Life camps at Winona Lake, Indiana.

ABOVE LEFT: College Church members worked on behalf of many community causes. Mrs. L. B. Wood (right), a member of the League of Women Voters, stands beside the League's entry in Wheaton's 1932 Fourth of July parade.

MAY THE BLESSING OF GOD THE FATHER, THE PEACE OF HIS SON, AND COMFORT OF HIS HOLY SPIRIT ABIDE WITH YOU THROUGH

the NEW YEAR

ALGERIA TUNIS

LIBYA EGYPT

"PRAYING ALWAYS WITH ALL PRAYER AND SUPPLI-CATION IN THE SPIRIT .....FOR ALL SAINTS AND FOR US THAT UTTERANCE MAY BE GIVEN TO US THAT WE MAY OPEN OUR MOUTHS BOLDLY, TO MAKE KNOWN THE MYS-TERY OF THE GOSPEL, FOR WHICH WE ARE AMBASSADORS" *Eph.* 6:18,19

UNION OF SOUTH AFRICA

MR. and MRS. PAUL P. STOUGH

AFRICA INLAND MISSION RETHI, ABA, CONGO BELGE via SUDAN, AFRICA

LEFT: Paul Stough and Rachel Winsor Stough were College Church young people who served under the Africa Inland Mission in the Belgian Congo. For several years, College Church provided full support for Rachel Stough and her sister-in-law, Mary Park Winsor. Stough spent one furlough (1946–1947) as interim pastor of College Church.

Courtesy of College Church in Wheaton

TOP: College Church members built a new church across from the college and worshiped in the new sanctuary from 1935 to 1993.

ABOVE LEFT: Evan Welsh (1933–1946) emphasized evangelism, spiritual growth, and missions during his pastorate. He later became chaplain at Wheaton College (1955–1970).

ABOVE RIGHT: Robert Rayburn (1947–1950) served as a chaplain in World War II and Korea. Popular with the young people, Pastor Rayburn initiated the first missionary conference at College Church.

LEFT: Dr. Carl Armerding (1951–1955), professor of Bible and theology at Wheaton College, took a leave of absence for full-time leadership at College Church.

ABOVE: Dr. L. P. "Dexter" McClenny (1958–1972) and his wife, Jane, who died in a car accident in 1966.

RIGHT: Nathan Goff (1973–1977), a Gordon-Conwell graduate, was called from Richview Baptist Church in Toronto.

BELOW: Olena Mae Welsh, Evan Welsh's second wife, joined the staff of College Church after her husband died, working especially with STARS. She developed strategies for providing support for parents of the intellectually and developmentally disabled.

Kent and Barbara Hughes (1979–2006). Pastor Hughes introduced the congregation to "serial Bible exposition" during his twenty-seven years of leadership.

College Church members dedicated a new sanctuary in 1993.

judge. Known as "Judge Penney," the new pastor was a gifted teacher, and the congregation embraced his ministry.

"I am not a faddist," Penney declared, "and am not inclined to specialize on any particular doctrine of the Bible. The fundamental facts of salvation through Christ are sufficient for me." At the end of 1931, Penney's health broke again. After major surgery in Chicago, he returned to Florida to recuperate. In September 1932, he died in Florida. The pulpit, vacant since December 1931, remained vacant through all of 1932. Herbert Moule and other college faculty filled in, assisted by occasional visiting preachers and missionaries.

Within two weeks of its organization, the Interdenominational Church presented College Church with a list of more than a hundred people who requested to withdraw from membership. The church responded on July 2, 1929, with a letter to each one on the list. Declaring the division "not only a reproach on the name of the Church and the College, but on the name of our Common Lord," the letter affirmed that College Church continued to stand "staunchly for every Fundamental of the Faith. But our orthodoxy counts for nothing," it continued, "unless we possess, and show the world that we possess, that union with Him which ensures union with His in Him."

A change in the membership process

The schism complicated the long association between College Church and Wheaton College. In the fall, both congregations courted returning students. President Buswell attended the Wheaton College Interdenominational Church, while most Wheaton College faculty continued to worship at College Church. In September, the two churches temporarily set aside their differences to promote the college's annual special services, which in 1929 featured the veteran Baptist preacher A. F. Purkiss.

Special services typically ran over two Sundays and required the spacious auditorium of the new chapel.

As College Church leaders sorted their membership list, President Buswell addressed a startling letter to the membership. He proposed that the two congregations select a mutually acceptable pastor but conduct their business and finances separately; a joint membership committee would visit and invite unchurched people. Those who came would then choose which group to join. College Church objected to this plan: it would have precluded unity by keeping differences in focus, and instead the church reorganized its membership process.

From 1930, it was possible for members of College Church to choose individually whether or not to associate with the Congregational National Convention. The church's financial obligations to the Illinois Congregational Association were calculated by the total denominational membership. The church remained a full member of the Association with full representation in its decision-making bodies, but at the same time, it functioned as an independent church for people who so preferred. Most members stood up to be counted as Congregationalists, but new members, especially those from other traditions, occasionally opted out. At the 1933 annual meeting, for example, the church reported 8 nondenominational and 332 denominational members.

President Buswell tried again in 1931 to heal the rift on his own terms, this time proposing that joint services be under the full control of Wheaton College. College Church countered with a suggestion for united Sunday evening services planned by a committee representing both congregations. After 1931, each congregation went its own way without further attempts to reunite.

For the moment, then, The College Church of Christ claimed its Congregationalist heritage without compromising its principles. When Congregationalists did effect a merger in 1931, it involved no Universalists: rather, the Congregational National Convention absorbed the General Convention of Christian Churches, itself an amalgam of several small regional networks with roots in revivals. The College Church of Christ raised no objections. It survived another crisis and held for a while longer the historic Congregational ties that had long influenced its identity.

CHAPTER 4

TRANSITIONS

We have heard the joyful sound,
Jesus saves! Jesus saves!
Spread the tidings all around,
Jesus saves! Jesus saves!
Bear the news to every land,
Climb the steeps and cross the waves,
Onward, 'tis our Lord's command;
Jesus saves! Jesus saves!

PRISCILLA OWENS, 1892

DESPITE THE DEPRESSION, the 1930s were good years for College Church. The church split in 1929 removed simmering discontent associated with fundamentalist separatism and allowed the two factions to pursue their priorities in their own ways. The members who remained with The College Church of Christ resolved to guard their spirits. They recognized that College Church could not thrive if its members harbored bitterness, and they determined not to involve students in "unedifying criticism or controversy." The recent abolition of the long-standing college requirement that students attend College Church meant that students were free to choose between the two campus congregations. It made rivalry and criticism real possibilities: the church split had the potential to divide the student body.

A week after the June 4, 1929, vote that split College Church, the congregation named a Friendly Relations Committee to make recommendations about relations with the splinter group. The committee brought its first report to a special business meeting on Wednesday evening, July 17, 1929. The report took the high road and set the tone for the next decade, calling on members to heed their own failings rather than those of others. "Central in the thought and plans of the church," the committee insisted, must be "the exaltation of Christ. With our minds centered on this, other things will be seen in their true proportions." The committee encouraged everyone to be more diligent in serving Christ through the church and urged them to covet the ability "to rejoice in the blessings which attend any and all other groups of God's children" and to avoid "discussing what appear to be the faults in others; rather, to discern and eliminate our own."

Pastor Evan Welsh

A new era began in 1933 with the arrival of Evan Welsh. Since the church split, the congregation had not had strong pastoral leadership, and people were eager for change. The second son of former pastor John Welsh, Evan Welsh graduated from Wheaton College in 1927 with a history major. During his student days, he was active in College Church and popular around town. On campus he was captain of the football team, a debater, and a prominent member of the Celts, one of the literary societies that structured campus social life. Upon graduation from Wheaton, he enrolled at Princeton Seminary, where his studies coincided with the stormy controversies that led to the founding of Westminster Seminary.

In 1929, Welsh accepted a call to a Presbyterian church on the edge of the campus of the University of Minnesota at Minneapolis. (Presbyterian ordination required four years of college and two of seminary, with the understanding that those who chose not to graduate from seminary would follow a recommended course of readings to complete their studies. Welsh exercised this option.) In September 1929, Welsh married his Wheaton College classmate Evangeline Mortenson at College Church, and they began ministry in the struggling Minneapolis Bethany Presbyterian Church, a congregation the presbytery had considered closing down. The Welshes had a heart for students, and they put the church back on its feet. They introduced college students to ministry at the Union City Mission and the city jail. Fellow clergy elected Evan Welsh president of the Union of Presbyterian Ministers of Minneapolis; he served as well on his denomination's national committee on evangelism and was a popular speaker at the Northwestern Bible Conference at Medicine Lake (where his father, John Welsh, and William Bell Riley were prominent), all before he reached the age of thirty.

When they agreed to return to Wheaton and to The College Church of Christ in 1933, the Welshes left a promising future in their denomination for a different set of connections with its own politics. They knew the challenges ahead. Wheaton was home to both of their families. Evangeline Mortenson Welsh's parents moved to Wheaton in 1922 so that she and her sisters, Margaret and Elizabeth, could attend Wheaton College. The family became active at College Church. Margaret Mortenson married Kenneth Landon, and the couple served as missionaries to Thailand. Margaret gained fame as the author of *Anna and the King of Siam*, the basis for the 1951 Broadway musical *The King and I*. Elizabeth Mortenson married the Rev. Donald Wayne Amsler, a Presbyterian pastor.

The excitement and confidence College Church members expressed as they anticipated Evan Welsh's leadership was remarkable. Welsh was twenty-seven, and the congregation still included some aged pioneers—people like professors D. A. Straw and Elsie Dow and Nettie Lumry, whose roots reached back to the Wesleyan Church before Jonathan Blanchard arrived in 1860. It had as well an atypical complement of seasoned ministers and missionaries, women as well as men. And with the recent split, the Welshes knew and respected people from both churches. On the surface, a call to College Church in 1933 had little to commend it to a young pastor whose church was prospering. The enthusiasm with which College Church embraced Evan Welsh testified to the high regard for him as well as to an eagerness to make a fresh start in a difficult time.

College Church's senior members were perhaps the most affirming, and the humility and grace with which he walked among them enabled Welsh to lead. Among the pressing immediate concerns were implementing a new relationship to Wheaton College that was faithful to College Church's original vision; learning to work easily and cordially with the college personnel active in Wheaton College Interdenominational Church; and perhaps most urgently, nurturing Christ-centered piety and a passion for souls in a congregation undergoing a difficult transition. From one perspective, when the congregation called Welsh, it took a calculated risk that paid rich dividends.

Finally, a building of its own

A few months after Welsh arrived, another concern was added to the list: the college gave the church the stipulated two years' notice and required it to vacate the chapel in the fall of 1935. In the mid-1930s, the real value of the church's investment in the building declined sharply. The church had no building fund other than what it would realize from liquidating its investment. But the college enrollment climbed during President Buswell's tenure, and the academic program thrived; the college anticipated needing more space, and the matter of two congregations meeting on campus also demanded resolution. By calling a pastor who understood and valued the long relationship between church and college, College Church reaffirmed its commitment to the campus community despite the need to move away.

The church resolved to relocate close enough to campus to sustain a vital program of student ministries. It acquired land on Washington Street–across the street from the west side of the college and just a block south of its former campus home. A building committee was formed, and a building fund grew slowly. The first year's receipts in cash and pledges totaled nearly $3,250. Sunday school building fund offerings added another $300, and the sale of an old Communion set netted an additional $4.33. The college met its obligations, members pitched in, and in 1935, a new sanctuary rose. A church house next door provided office and Sunday school rooms that the college used during the week as overflow classroom space. The building was dedicated in November 1935 with Louis Evans preaching. The son of former pastor William Evans and a graduate of Wheaton Academy, Louis Evans was a rising star among Northern Presbyterians. He graduated from McCormick Theological Seminary and in 1935 was pastor of Pittsburgh's 1,700-member Third Presbyterian Church. The evening before the dedication, Evan Welsh quietly opened the new sanctuary with a Communion service.

The new College Church building cost just over $60,000. The church's investment in the college chapel brought $43,000, and a mortgage covered most of the remainder. In May 1939, the loan was paid off and the mortgage burned. The costs associated with furnishing the building exceeded estimates, but the congregation contributed money and labor and made cash payments on time. Funds were ample, and neither home nor global outreaches suffered.

Once the congregation settled into its new home, each Sunday worship bulletin carried a picture of the church and these words of welcome: "To all in need of a Saviour, to all seeking spiritual help and guidance, to all who would worship the only true God, we extend a welcome to worship with us, praying that God may use every service for his glory and the upbuilding of his Kingdom." The congregation presented itself as a blend of people from many denominations united around "the great fundamentals of the gospel," and it welcomed to membership "those of like faith." Evan Welsh wrote in 1944, "It is a happy fellowship representing many denominational backgrounds." Longtime member and professor Elsie Dow reaffirmed the church's ongoing heart for the campus:

> The constant influx of new life, we recognize as our great opportunity and responsibility, while at the same time we are strengthened and gladdened by many of these young servants of the Lord whose zeal to avail themselves of some at least of the many avenues of service open to them is an inspiration to us all. May we continue and increase in this fellowship of mutual service, blessing and being blest, never forgetting that we serve the Lord Christ!

Space became a problem almost as soon as the new building opened. The auditorium could comfortably accommodate 600 and seat 630 "with the aid of a shoe horn and much persuasion," but higher attendance required extra chairs. Within a few years, average Sunday morning attendance during the school year exceeded 630. Professors Herbert Moule and Elsie Dow began a children's church in the church house next door to alleviate crowding, and an overflow service of longtime members met in the church basement to make room for visitors in the sanctuary.

Growth in church programs

Evan Welsh had a keen sense of calling that expressed itself in various ways. He studied for five hours every morning, made himself available to everyone during specified office hours five afternoons a week, and then devoted himself to visitation. He reported in 1937 that he had made 1,400 pastoral calls on members in the past year. On Friday evenings he enlisted men from the congregation to make visits with him. He loved people and delighted in this face-to-face, personal work. Occasionally he shared with the church council informal lists of the people he knew had acknowledged Christ as Savior within the year. The lists showed that he considered any time and any place an appropriate setting for Christian witness. The list for 1937 included eighty people he had led to faith in places that ranged from a Glen Ellyn gas station to a Naperville tuberculosis sanitarium to private homes and his own study.

Sunday was THE LORD'S DAY, noted as such on every monthly church calendar, generally in bold caps. Welsh's choice of attire as well as the order of service underscored his reverence for the written and spoken Word. Corporate worship was all about spending time in the presence of the One who gave "overcoming power and eternal life to all who trust in Him." Whatever the weather, summer and winter, Welsh delivered his Sunday sermons in formal attire. He processed in with the choir during the singing of the first hymn. The congregation stood for the hymn, the doxology, the invocation, and the *Gloria*. Traditional hymns, a responsive reading, a choral anthem, and a vocal solo preceded the sermon. Communion was celebrated every other month. A verse such as Habakkuk 2:20 stood at the head of the weekly bulletin: "The LORD is in his holy temple: let all the earth keep silence before him." "Our worship begins with the first note of the organ," the congregation read. "May we make the prelude a period of special prayer for the service."

Evening services included a choir hymn and featured a gospel song service accompanied by an orchestra. During the school year, bulletins often invited the congregation to conclude the Lord's Day at a "formal Back Home Sing" hosted by Mr. and

Mrs. Evan Welsh. Perhaps ten times each year, Welsh asked someone else to fill the pulpit Sunday morning or evening. He attended, but he wanted to expose the congregation to other styles of preaching than his own.

A zeal for missions and for evangelism

Despite the deepening Depression, the congregation expanded its efforts on many fronts. During 1934–the last year the congregation met at the college chapel–the Women's Missionary Society held twenty-one regular meetings and several special functions. Women contributed a penny a day to the Society, heard from home and foreign missionaries–including an African American missionary working in Chicago under the American Missionary Association–and participated with other women's missionary societies in special projects. Their slogan was "A penny and a prayer a day for missions."

Evangeline Welsh took hold of the Christian Endeavor meetings with a vision for enlisting every young person in the "active ranks." Chalk talks, Bible studies, and consecration services drew a steady group to the Junior Christian Endeavor. High school students attended Intermediate Christian Endeavor, where they took responsibility for a weekly program and sponsored one consecration service and one missionary service each month. College Christian Endeavor was the largest of the three Endeavor groups, and it, too, featured worship, consecration, missions, and evangelistic outreaches. One Sunday each month, the college group set aside its Christian Endeavor program in favor of a Singspiration.

The Fishermen's Club offered fellowship over meals, devotional exercises, and gospel work. Members distributed thousands of tracts and gospels and shared their personal testimonies with gratifying results. Gospel teams recruited people to add their names to a list of those willing to go where opportunity beckoned. When meetings were scheduled, teams of five or six, chosen from the list, undertook various forms of witness. Church members provided transportation. A typical team included a pianist, a song leader, a speaker, and two or three others. Teams took regular responsibility for rescue mission services three Saturday nights each month. In the 1930s they held regular weekly services at two nearby Civilian Conservation Corps camps, one in Warrenville and one on St. Charles Road near Elmhurst.

The Civilian Conservation Corps was formed during newly elected president Franklin D. Roosevelt's first "Hundred Days," part of his New Deal relief program. Established by Congress, the program hired young, unskilled workers from families on relief to work on conservation projects. The typical camp accommodated fifty men, most between eighteen and twenty years of age, who signed on for six months of work, forty hours per week, for $30 per month. Food, clothing, and medical care were provided, and much of the wage was sent to the worker's dependants. College Church young people seized the opportunity to reach out to this mobile group of people their own age. They interacted as well with students at the local Williams Military Academy (later to become the Midwest Military Academy).

Each year, women's missionary circles conducted ten monthly meetings and nine evening "sociables," packed barrels of clothing, sewed for places as varied as Fuchow Hospital in China and the College Church kitchen, followed a course of reading, and collected items to distribute among needy families. The missionary committee sponsored a missionary prayer meeting each month, and sometimes missionaries on furlough brought firsthand information to the congregation. The relief committee reported sufficient funds to meet worthy requests. Jail work proceeded with the assistance of college students. Every

Sunday morning, College Church staffed a morning service at the DuPage County Jail; later an evening gospel song service was added.

Besides Christian Endeavor and outreach efforts, college students networked through a young people's camp in Elgin, hymn sings, student holiday socials, and a monthly publication called *The Ambassador*. Deaconesses devoted themselves to calling on the sick, visiting shut-ins, and welcoming new families to the community, making hundreds of calls each year. College Church men organized as the Brotherhood and met frequently for inspirational and social programs. Deacons reported regularly that the church had more than met expenses: all its bills were paid. The elders, meanwhile, made calls in the interest of keeping Wheaton dry, participated in the time-consuming work of planning for the future, and joined Evan Welsh in Friday evening "calling nights." The venerable D. A. Straw, chair of the elders in 1934, gave thanks for "a most intimate, peaceful, and unified fellowship in Christ which keeps our hearts aglow and has been cherished with constant persistent prayer together for continued blessing."

During Evan Welsh's pastorate, most annual reports included words like the following from 1942: "We are aware that the greatest single human factor responsible for the church's spiritual growth during the past year has been our faithful pastor. His own response to the call of our times has been communicated to us all. As we face the new year with all its uncertainties, may we as never before respond to our pastor's challenge to join him in giving the gospel to our community and to the world."

Evan Welsh's years as pastor showed heartening results as the congregation united behind him in worship, outreach, and giving. Yet all was not sweetness and light. Relationships with the college required wisdom, especially as the church learned to deal with the loss of its privileged relationship to students.

From 1929 through 1935, College Church united with Wheaton College Interdenominational Church for the annual spring and fall evangelistic services as well as for special events. In fact, because the college's largest meeting space doubled as College Church's sanctuary, College Church was obligated to host the splinter congregation. When both moved off campus, each needed to promote itself to students.

Among other things, College Church printed a flyer for student mailboxes that featured the school colors–bright orange and blue–and introduced Evan Welsh as "a former letter-lineman on the Wheaton grid team . . . now in the line on the victory side for Christ." The church hosted regular student roundtables that drew some two hundred students. College professors and other professionals offered at least seven different college Sunday school classes. For a few years, tennis player live-wire Alan Cheesebro led the College Christian Endeavor while college debater Ralph Clough and other presidents of the Young People's Council kept the youth program responsive to student interests. Welsh believed that students were best served by "the normal program of an active and 'fundamental' church home," a family church that integrated them fully into congregational life. He strove for a "vital personal contact" with each student, and the church provided social as well as spiritual and service opportunities that took the campus calendar into account.

Victorious Life conferences

In 1933, College Church began sponsoring Victorious Life conferences at Winona Lake, Indiana. These summer events drew a cross section of the congregation several hundred strong for time apart to concentrate on personal piety. The teaching featured the themes popularized by the Keswick Movement. Begun in England in 1875, annual conventions at Keswick in England's Lake District drew transatlantic audiences for programs that emphasized experiencing the transforming power of Christ within. Keswick hymnals elaborated the convention's message of full salvation. The victorious life began with an act of the will:

> *Let in the Overcomer, and he will conquer thee.*
> *Thy broken spirit taken in sweet captivity*
> *Shall glory in his triumph and share his victory.*

Lines from the era's gospel hymns spoke to the consequences of "letting the Overcomer in": by "constantly abiding" and taking Christ "moment by moment," believers could experience the victorious Christianity they professed. Hannah Whitall Smith's best-selling book *The Christian's Secret of a Happy Life* popularized the Keswick message, and Frances Ridley Havergal provided the signature Keswick hymn:

> *Like a river glorious is God's perfect peace,*
> *Over all victorious in its bright increase;*
> *Perfect, yet it groweth fuller every day,*
> *Perfect, yet it floweth deeper all the way.*
>
> *Stayed upon Jehovah hearts are fully blest,*
> *Finding, as he promised, perfect peace and rest.*

Perfect, yet growing fuller–perfect, yet flowing deeper–such phrases summoned Christians to grow in Christ, and Christ-centered spiritual growth headed Evan Welsh's list of the things he coveted most for College Church. He yearned to know "what it really means to follow the Lord who gave himself for us." Beside this priority stood evangelism. "Oh, the compensations for [evangelism]," he wrote in 1940. "The unspeakable joy of seeing Christ formed in the hungry hearts one finds. . . . In these dark, dark times, I am so anxious that we as a church shall shine as brightly as he would have us in the night of sin."

College Church of Christ had long since abandoned Jonathan Blanchard's distaste for Christmas celebrations, and the tradition of Christmas pageants and choral celebrations was well established. The Christmas season concluded with two festive events: a Watch Night service from 9:00 p.m. until midnight on New Year's Eve and a New Year's Day dinner prepared under the auspices of the church social committee.

On December 7, 1941, the College Church sponsored its usual activities. Wheaton College student Billy Graham spoke to the College Christian Endeavor, and the evening evangelistic service proceeded as planned.

The next morning, Wheaton citizens learned that eight young men from the town were stationed in Hawaii when the Japanese bombs fell on Pearl Harbor. One went down with the USS *Arizona*, another was on the USS *Enterprise*, and several others were stationed at Hickam Air Force Base in Honolulu. On December 8, Wheaton men began enlisting: the first two—one of them the brother of the sailor lost on the *Arizona*—joined the navy. Amid growing preoccupation with international affairs, the College Church congregation planned its year-end programs. The church council met on December 9 and recessed to hear President Roosevelt's address to the nation before completing its business.

An unexpected tragedy

Between Christmas and New Year's Eve, Evan and Evangeline Welsh drove to Indiana for a brief family visit. As they traveled home in the early morning hours of December 31, their car hit a patch of ice, Evan Welsh lost control of the vehicle, and they skidded into the path of an oncoming pickup truck. His wife died instantly, and her mother had to be cut from the vehicle by emergency responders. Evan Welsh and those in the truck were injured less severely. That morning, the headline in the *Wheaton Daily Journal* read, "Wheaton Pastor's Wife Dies." The city's population hovered around 8,500, and the community shared the congregation's shocked sense of loss.

College Church members gathered as usual for the Watch Night service but cancelled the annual New Year's dinner. Evan Welsh returned to Wheaton on January 2, and on Saturday, January 3, Moody Church pastor Harry Ironside conducted Evangeline Welsh's funeral. The Welshes had two daughters, Joan and Mary, nine and five years old. The next day was Sunday, and the morning sermon at College Church by the Rev. Thomas Lindsay addressed the topic "All things work together for good." The next week, Evan Welsh returned to his pulpit to preach "This Is the Victory." He called his evening sermon "New Lives for Old." (In April 1966, another College Church pastor's wife, Jane McClenny, died in an automobile accident. Jane and Dexter McClenny were en route from Wheaton to Kentucky to visit a high school missions team when he lost control of the vehicle on a wet road.)

Expanding emphasis on missions

During the difficult years of the Depression and World War II, College Church expanded its commitments to home and foreign missions. The focus of home missionary work had changed with the society: needs and circumstances after World War I demanded different forms of involvement. Contributions to Congregational societies kept the church involved in supporting African American education in the South, but proportionally more funds were directed to places like the Union Gospel League, Moody Bible Institute, or the Pacific Garden Mission.

The church continued its long history of contributions to the American Board of Commissioners for Foreign Missions as well as to individual ABCFM missionaries, but a growing number of its missionaries now served under other denominations or the newer faith missionary agencies like the China Inland Mission, Africa Inland Mission, or the Christian and Missionary Alliance.

In January 1928, College Church began a long and close relationship with the Paul Stough family, missionaries serving in the Belgian Congo under the Africa Inland Mission. (Like her sister-in-law, Mary Park Winsor, in the 1930s, Rachel Stough received full support from College Church.)

At a church council meeting in October 1937, the commitment to financial involvement in missions was discussed. Despite the Depression, giving to missions had actually increased: by July 1937, College Church had received as much for missions as during the entire previous year. After a series of reports, Evan Welsh proposed that the church should strive for a missions budget that equaled or exceeded its home budget. The discussion led to a resolution that has guided the church since: "Resolved, that it is the definite purpose and aim of the Church Council of the College Church of Christ for our church to have our missionary gifts equal or in excess of our home expenses." It took the congregation until 1954 to achieve parity for the first time: the budget that year allotted just over $27,000 each to work at home and abroad. Budgets regularly approach parity, but in recent years only three have realized it. In 2010, missions giving approached $3 million while the rest of the church budget stood at $3.2 million.

In 1939, the church purchased a parsonage at 707 N. Washington Street in Wheaton. The congregation made its last payment on the parsonage in 1942, and leaders once again began looking toward the future. Increased attendance made it necessary to rent college classrooms for the Sunday school, and some classes reported "standing room only." The membership totaled 884. Well over a hundred young men from the church had been drafted, but regular canvasses of new residents drew in more worshipers. Former interim pastor Professor Herbert Moule chaired the evangelism committee and kept the congregation busy with outreach. A new building committee looked ahead: the church designated the first Sunday of each month for receiving building fund pledges.

Wartime rationing took its toll on gospel work and on church socials. Gospel teams gave up much of their work in Chicago in favor of closer opportunities that required less rubber and gas. Mission Sunday schools flourished on Sunday afternoons on Jewell Road and in the southeast and southwest sections of town; Evan Welsh conducted the one on the southwest side. A week of special meetings with the young evangelist Torrey Johnson drew a record Sunday school attendance of 979, and twenty new members brought the church family to 904. Pastor Welsh considered volunteering as an army chaplain, and the church council designated a student pastor to assist with student ministries in Welsh's anticipated absence. The war ended before Welsh's appointment came through, and the student pastor stayed on at lower pay as a pastoral assistant. For several years, Welsh and the elders wrote weekly letters to service personnel. When the volume of correspondence overwhelmed the short-staffed church office, volunteers stepped up to keep the letters going out.

Struggling with Denominational Affiliation

During World War II, an energetic group of conservative Protestants acted to reclaim evangelicalism's place on the American religious landscape, and from the start, College Church members supported their efforts. Fundamentalists had earned a reputation as fighters and separatists; a new generation of conservative Protestants preferred to focus on proclamation and united action with those who shared their core beliefs. They wanted a place at the table in national conversations that touched on faith and public life. In 1942 in St. Louis, a group of 147 conservative Protestants established the National Association of Evangelicals (NAE). In 1943, The College Church of Christ voted to join the NAE. The church also encouraged the early ministry of Billy Graham, a Wheaton College graduate who would soon become the most recognizable face of a new evangelicalism.

Growing interest in making common cause with other evangelicals corresponded to a mounting sense that affiliation with the Congregational Christian Churches was little more than a vestige of the past. Wheaton College no longer had a strong complement of Congregational faculty or trustees, and over the years, the ordained Congregationalists on College Church's rolls had died or moved away. The Congregational churches with which College Church had enjoyed long relationships were under new leadership, and influential people in the Illinois Association sympathized with a theologically liberal trajectory that veered sharply from the congregation's priorities.

Congregational foreign missions looked different too. In 1932, a widely publicized multidenominational Protestant self-study brought the entire Protestant missionary enterprise into question and laid bare stark differences between liberals and conservatives. *Re-thinking Missions: A Layman's Inquiry After 100 Years* (1932) proposed new approaches to overseas missionary endeavors that had less to do with proclaiming an exclusive message than with promoting human welfare. The ABCFM participated in the general reassessment of missionary goals, and College Church could not endorse its new direction. Nor did members approve the new secretary of the Illinois Association, a man whose beliefs on some points were known to differ sharply from the church's Articles of Faith. The congregation registered its protest with the Association and during the 1940s began considering its options.

The Congregational Christian Churches participated fully in the ecumenical movement that gathered momentum before World War II, and in 1940 it began merger talks with the Evangelical and Reformed Church, itself a merger of small German Reformed associations. All parties had long-standing ecumenical commitments, but the journey to the union that in 1957 created the United Church of Christ took seventeen years and sharply divided Congregationalists. At stake was the cherished full autonomy of local congregations.

In 1946, a new College Church Manual revised the wording that described College Church's evolving relationship to its denomination. "The church maintains a fundamental witness in the denomination," it read, "but is entirely independent in its program and missionary giving." The new Manual also explained that College Church had no ties to the Federal Council of the Churches of Christ, the premier American ecumenical association; rather, it was an active member of the NAE. Pastor Welsh pointed out that this claim would be strictly true only if the church withdrew from the Congregational Association. Otherwise, a portion of its giving went to its denomination-supported ecumenical endeavors. A few conservative churches had already broken their ties to state Congregational associations–for instance, Park Street Church in Boston and Lake Avenue Congregational Church in Pasadena, California–and College Church considered following their examples and becoming an independent evangelical Congregational church.

In 1948, the elders investigated thoroughly the implications of withdrawal, and they brought the matter to the congregation for vote in March 1948. The church approved the following resolution and elected two women and three men as its representatives to the next meeting of the Illinois Association:

Resolved, that College Church of Christ go on record as disapproving the proposed union of the Congregational Christian Churches and the Evangelical and Reformed Church in a body to be known as the United Church of Christ, and that the vote of this church be cast to that effect by regularly appointed representatives at the proper time and place.

Be it further resolved that the College Church of Christ respectfully declares that should such a union be consummated, it will not in any manner whatsoever enter into or become part of such union or the United Church of Christ, or adhere thereto, or become responsible to or for the same.

In the end, College Church did not wait for the merger to be finalized. The denomination's direction was clear, and College Church exercised its right to withdraw from the Association. Its last listing in the *Congregational Christian Year Book* appeared in 1947. In 1929, J. Oliver Buswell had tried to force the issue and split the Association with the result that he split the church. Twenty years later, the time was right—no members dissented, and the church did not stir up strife in the Association.

Post-War Activities

The process of disengaging from the denomination occurred amid other changes. In the spring of 1946, Evan Welsh resigned the pastorate to accept a call to Ward Memorial Presbyterian Church in Detroit. He left in May, and in November the elders reported that twenty-nine different people had filled the pulpit since. The congregation turned to furloughing Africa missionary Paul Stough to provide continuity while it searched for a pastor. It soon found one of its own—Robert G. Rayburn, a 1935 graduate of Wheaton College, who was just completing an army chaplaincy in Europe (where he served 1944–1946).

A graduate of Dallas Seminary, Rayburn served College Church until 1950, when he was called to active duty in the Korean War. He led the congregation during the process of withdrawal from Congregational affiliation. Also during his tenure, the church announced its first annual missionary conference. There had been many prior services with a strong missions emphasis, but this one proposed to initiate a new tradition. The conference met from Thursday, January 29, through Sunday, February 1, 1948, with eight missionaries in attendance. At the time, College Church of Christ provided full support to four missionary units: the Paul Stough family in the Belgian Congo; Clayton Howard at HCJB in Quito, Ecuador; and the Donald Stark family and Nancy Carpenter, serving with Wycliffe Bible Translators in Peru. The church partially supported eighteen others as well.

As the troops returned home from their involvement in World War II, the College Church Brotherhood kept alive the old impulse to cooperate with other Wheaton churches for the common good. The church had representatives on the Christian Layman's Committee of Wheaton. In 1948, they undertook a citywide canvass, interviewing 6,438 family units. They discovered 426 with no church affiliation or preference, and these were the people they worked to enlist. The College Church Keystone Fellowship offered a place of service for young people who provided Bibles for boys at Williams Military Academy; conducted a Sunday school north of Glen Ellyn on Sunday afternoons; assisted at a Sunday school on the south side of Chicago; volunteered at the Gospel League Shelter for Women in Chicago; and otherwise kept themselves busy in evangelistic work. Each week during Pastor Rayburn's tenure, members of the Fishermen's Club gathered at 7:30 on Saturday evenings to pray for the Sunday services.

Two Sunday morning services now alleviated crowding in the sanctuary. Average attendance was 301 at the 9:45 service and 396 at the 11:00 service. The average attendance at Sunday school increased from 368 in 1948 to 423 the next year. These annual averages, of course, did not fully capture the seasonal bustle of activity during the college year.

Pastor Rayburn was highly esteemed, especially among young people, who enjoyed his stories of wartime adventures. When he left for Korea, he continued his adventures as chaplain with the paratroopers of the 187th Airborne. The *Wheaton Daily Journal* reported his jumps (without training) into combat zones. After the Korean War, Rayburn took a prominent role in what became the Presbyterian Church in America (PCA). A pastor and a college and seminary president (Covenant Seminary in St. Louis), he died in 1990.

Rayburn's departure from College Church in 1950 marked the end of the era that had begun with Evan Welsh's arrival in 1933. Evan Welsh had eased the transition from campus church to community church with a campus emphasis. His pastorate brought stability and set in place the programs and outreaches that prepared College Church to be a fully independent evangelical congregation. He stamped his passion for evangelism on the foreign missions program and on local relationships, and when he left, The College Church of Christ was networked with the new evangelical parachurch organizations that channeled the energies of the next generation of leaders. Robert Rayburn saw the process of denominational disaffiliation through to completion and kept enthusiasm high. On his departure in 1950, College Church seemed poised for a bright future.

CHAPTER 5

CHARACTERISTICS

I love thy kingdom, Lord,
The house of thine abode,
The church our blest Redeemer saved
With his own precious blood.

TIMOTHY DWIGHT, 1800

ON SATURDAY, FEBRUARY 19, 1955, the *Wheaton Daily Journal* devoted a full page to College Church. "College Church of Christ Parallels Wheaton Growth," the banner headline announced. Wheaton was growing, and the church was about to expand its facilities again. Overcrowding had drawn the congregation back to its former home: during the school year, it rented the college's Pierce Chapel for Sunday morning services. The college and church regularly took advantage of proximity and used each other's space, but now the congregation anticipated acting on its long-deferred plans to build an education wing. The prospering and expanding church mirrored a national trend.

Religious participation was strong in the Cold War years following World War II: Americans juxtaposed godless communism with faith, adding "under God" to the Pledge of Allegiance in 1954 and adopting "in God we trust" as the national motto in 1956. People flocked to Billy Graham crusades and tuned in to

Fulton J. Sheen on radio and television, while books by Norman Vincent Peale were national best sellers. After lagging during the Depression and the War, church construction skyrocketed, and liturgical renewal enriched worship.

Pastors Armerding, Lazear, McClenny, and Goff

By 1951 The College Church of Christ averaged 875 on Sunday mornings and 425 in the evenings. The Sunday school enrolled 600. Already in 1951, the church extended its basement to accommodate its need for classrooms. In 1952, it purchased the lot immediately to its south for $20,000. Plans under consideration in 1955 envisioned a 1,000-seat auditorium in addition to rooms for Sunday school classes and youth activities, as well as a gymnasium. The plans proved too ambitious for the times, but even a modest expansion alleviated crowding.

Dr. Carl Armerding, energetic president of the Central American Mission, a missionary-sending agency, had been pastor since 1951. Armerding had also been a professor of Bible and theology at Wheaton College, but he was now on leave from Wheaton's faculty in order to carry out his pastoral responsibilities. Working alongside Armerding was the congregation's first full-time associate pastor of record, the Rev. Kenneth E. Churchill, whose missionary service with the China Inland Mission had come to an abrupt end with communist victories in China's civil war. Churchill's duties were administration and visitation, and while he served the church, he completed a degree at Wheaton College (1957). Carl Armerding, meanwhile, became pastor emeritus in 1955.

Such men cultivated the congregation's already considerable commitment to missions by word and example. Both had been missionaries, and Armerding served on various mission agency boards long after he retired from the pulpit. In 1951, the church provided substantial support to twenty missionaries, and connections with missionaries cultivated through the Women's Missionary Society extended the list by thirty-seven units. Armerding's successor, Robert Lazear, kept missionary enthusiasm high. Ordained in the Northern Presbyterian Church, Lazear (Wheaton College class of 1937) trained for the ministry at Princeton Seminary and Dallas Theological Seminary and went to Colombia in 1943 as a Presbyterian missionary. When he accepted the College Church pulpit in 1955, he intended to remain stateside indefinitely.

Within a year, however, the tug of missions proved irresistible. Intensifying persecution of Protestants in Colombia and the inability of new missionaries to obtain visas drew the Lazears back to South America. They knew the language and had return permits and connections that enabled them to easily resume the work they had left. Their departure for South America happened just after the widely publicized deaths on January 8, 1956, of five missionaries at the hands of the Auca Indians in Ecuador. (Three of the five–Jim Elliot, Nate Saint, and Ed McCully–were Wheaton College graduates.) During Lazear's brief tenure at College Church, plans to complete the education building were pushed forward.

Over more than a decade, several building committees had planned the expansion, but only in the late 1950s did the congregation have the will and resources to move ahead. The education wing rose behind the sanctuary and was dedicated on March 5, 1961. Pastor emeritus Carl Armerding prayed the dedicatory prayer, and the new pastor, Livius Poindexter (L. P.) McClenny, delivered a sermon entitled "Dedication Blessings." The new building provided up-to-date facilities for nurseries and Sunday school classes as well as for social and recreational pastimes, but it did not relieve crowding in the sanctuary. Leaders at nearby Christian ministries including Pioneer Girls, Scripture Press, and David C. Cook staffed youth programs such as Pioneer Girls, Boys' Brigade, and HYACKS (the church's high school youth group).

Pastor McClenny, his wife, and their four daughters had moved to Wheaton in 1958 from the Calvary Independent Presbyterian Church of Charlotte, North Carolina (where Franklin Graham, Billy Graham's father, was a founding elder). A graduate of Wheaton College (class of 1931), McClenny remained at College Church until 1972, becoming the longest-serving pastor to date. His son-in-law, John Dettoni, was the associate pastor during part of that time.

During Pastor McClenny's tenure, College Church members took an active role in planting a church in the new village of Carol Stream. Village Bible Church opened its doors in 1960 with support from College Church and several other Wheaton congregations.

In 1963, members of The College Church of Christ voted to change their name to College Church in Wheaton. They took this step to avoid confusion with the Churches of Christ, a denomination with different roots and traditions from their own. The leadership also reaffirmed the long-standing policy of requiring baptism for church membership.

In 1972, Pastor McClenny moved to Bibletown Community Church in Boca Raton, Florida, and the congregation called Nathan Goff, a Gordon-Conwell Seminary graduate, former pastor at Grace Chapel, Lexington, Massachusetts, and most recently on the staff of Richview Baptist Church in Toronto. Goff served for four years. He resigned in 1977, and once again a long list of able preachers filled the pulpit–John Stott, J. I. Packer, Wheaton College faculty, and leaders in the evangelical associations clustered around Wheaton.

Pastor Kent Hughes

In 1979, the pastoral search committee discovered R. Kent Hughes, a young California pastor whose abilities and vision they found appealing. The Hughes family accepted College Church's offer and moved to Wheaton in the fall of 1979. Associate pastor Larry Fullerton, on staff since 1976, brought a measure of continuity with the recent past.

Kent Hughes came to College Church from a Friends (Quaker) congregation, but his education at Talbot Theological Seminary had exposed him as well to the conservative evangelical world. Evangelical Friends were Arminian, while College Church had a long history of Congregational and Presbyterian pastors. Friends celebrated no church ordinances–Kent Hughes had never baptized anyone (though he had been baptized as an infant in a Presbyterian church), nor had he presided at Communion. After thorough interviews and examination of the candidate's theology, church leaders now assured members that Kent Hughes was a Calvinist with no reservations about church ordinances.

As the Hughes family took their places in the College Church family, Kent Hughes introduced the congregation to a style of preaching he called "serial Bible exposition." He moved methodically–and slowly–through entire books of the Bible, a practice he followed through twenty-seven years in the College Church pulpit. He believed that the application of the text was a work of the Holy Spirit, and so he did not encumber his preaching with practical applications. Hughes devoted himself to study; he developed into a preaching pastor, and as time passed, he came to rely on others to fulfill many aspects of ministry. He also set in place holiday traditions around Good Friday, Easter, Thanksgiving, and Christmas that became embedded in congregational life.

In 1980, College Church added a full-time college pastor in the person of Jerry Root, who had previously served with Kent Hughes in California. Larry Fullerton, meanwhile, moved into the role of executive/missions pastor. Marc Maillefer joined the staff as youth pastor. (He later became pastor for Christian education, then senior associate pastor, for a total of twenty-three years at College Church. Only Kent Hughes served the congregation longer than Maillefer.)

The next year, Kent Hughes took the first step toward making College Church a place for ministry training by instituting an internship program. Since 1981, more than two hundred people have received hands-on training as interns at College Church. A ministerial residency program (analogous to medical residency) was added in 2006. It provides funding for fully trained pastors to work for two years under the tutelage of seasoned ministers. In 1994, Kent Hughes hosted the first College Church Workshop on Biblical Exposition, an annual gathering designed to hone preachers' exegetical and expository skills.

In 2001, Hughes also became founding chairman of the Charles Simeon Trust, an independent organization committed to supporting gospel initiatives that include regional workshops on biblical exposition. Meanwhile Kent Hughes's wife, Barbara, launched a women's Bible study at the church, a weekly event that soon included hundreds of women from area churches and became, in Kent Hughes's estimation, the single most effective evangelistic outreach of his tenure at College Church. In 1987, the church approved a sabbatical program–six months of study leave after each seven years of service–for its expanding list of pastors.

A new sanctuary and expanded ministries

Late in the 1980s, as people responded to Kent Hughes's expository preaching, larger facilities again became a pressing need. Ground was broken on June 23, 1991, on land the church had first acquired in 1890 for a parsonage. It had changed hands several times and had been reacquired for parking space. Now it became the site of the church's new sanctuary. On January 31, 1993,

College Church dedicated a 1,000-seat auditorium connected to its original buildings but facing south instead of toward the Wheaton College campus to the east. Former Wheaton College President Hudson T. Armerding preached on "Fulfilling Our Calling," and Kent Hughes's mentor, Verl Lindley, prayed the dedicatory prayer. That evening, J. I. Packer preached a solemn message, "To the Church at Sardis" from Revelation 3:3–"Remember . . . how thou hast received and heard, and hold fast, and repent."

In the next year, attendance climbed sharply: Sunday morning attendance grew by 32 percent to 1,800, Sunday school records documented 27 percent growth, and giving was up 24 percent. A growing pastoral staff cultivated the new opportunities that followed. Young men worked under Kent Hughes for a few years and then moved on into their own pulpits. Women on the staff were ministry directors; men were pastors.

Among the women who carved out an enduring ministry space for themselves in these years was Olena Mae Welsh, the second wife and now widow of former pastor Evan Welsh. An eager worker, Welsh had a heart for special education and expanded the church's ministry to people with intellectual and developmental disabilities and their families. This program, now known as STARS (Seeking To Always Reflect the Savior), remains a definitive part of the congregation's identity and draws people from neighboring areas.

Behind the scenes in the 1990s, Kent Hughes led the staff and elders in evaluating College Church goals and ministries with an eye toward the new millennium. His 1996 sermon "Vision 2000: Ministry Countdown to the Next Millennium" set the tone by identifying seven essential values for a God-honoring congregation. They were not new, but by ordering them and relating them around a goal, Hughes gave them fresh meaning. By upholding these values–Christ, the Bible, balance, character, equipping, evangelism, and prayer–the congregation would press toward Christian maturity and would also be contagious about gospel and missions, well connected and cared for, committed to church planting, and involved in ministry training for Kingdom expansion. Three ministry priorities–characterized as upward, inward, outward–summarized the church's obligation to worship, nurture, evangelize, and bear social witness.

The staff prepared another document, "Pursuing Christ" (1996), which profiled Christian maturity and described the Christian life. The congregation embraced the Christ-centered, gospel-focused burden of Kent Hughes's ministry in a new church mission statement: "God's people joyfully proclaiming Christ's glory among the nations." In 1998, two College Church pastors acted on Kent Hughes's burden for church planting. With several College Church families, David Helm and Jon Dennis moved from Wheaton to Chicago to establish Holy Trinity Church. After more than a decade, Holy Trinity has multiple meeting sites, its own internship program, and an expanding vision for ministry in Chicago. Christ the King Church in Batavia (2001) and New Covenant Church in Naperville (2008) followed, and another plant is scheduled to open in Chicago's western suburbs in 2011.

In its long history, College Church had never before had a pastor who strove so consistently over so many years to integrate and evaluate every aspect of ministry around a single purpose. Part of the vision was another expansion of facilities to which the congregation turned soon after building its sanctuary. In 2000, College Church dedicated a 52,000-square-foot ministry center across the street from the church sanctuary. In addition to housing the church offices and church functions, this College Church Commons is the meeting place for a Liberian congregation.

Once again, worship space was at a premium–during the school year, first two, then three Sunday morning services were needed to accommodate the congregation. Youth programs thrived. Besides having a college pastor, the church added full-time youth pastors to work with junior and senior high students—the KMs (King's Messengers) and HYACKS. The missions program flourished, expanding to support two hundred career missionaries. Summer missions trips were added for high school students and STAMP (Short-Term Adult Missionary Program) was launched with the ambitious goal of enlisting at least half the congregation in short-term missionary work.

Kent Hughes's preaching, consistency, and vision brought wider visibility to the College Church pulpit. He contributed seventeen books to the Preaching the Word commentary series from Crossway Books and became the series general editor. Other books, especially *Disciplines of a Godly Man*, sold well. He served on the translation oversight committee for the best-selling English Standard Version (released in 2001) and on other boards and committees. His sabbaticals extended his networks to include Anglican evangelicals like Philip Jensen, Peter Jensen, P. T. O'Brien, Dick Lucas, Wallace Benson, and John Chapman. His academic interests and passion for the gospel brought him into association with D. A. Carson at Trinity Evangelical Divinity School.

The College Church congregation included stalwarts like Kenneth Taylor, founder of Tyndale House Publishers and the Christian Booksellers Association, whose biblical paraphrase, *The Living Bible* (1971), sold over forty million copies in North America alone and has since been translated into over one hundred languages. Other publishers were represented too—Joseph Bayly of David C. Cook; Lane Dennis of Good News Publishers/Crossway Books; staff from Scripture Press and Moody Publishers and Christianity Today International. In addition, the congregation included numerous missions executives, employees of the National Association of Evangelicals, and faculty from Moody Bible Institute and, of course, Wheaton College.

College Church members participated in worldwide associations that defined the new evangelicalism–they were leaders and support staff, and their connections enriched the congregation at the same time that Kent Hughes's publishing, teaching, traveling, training, church planting, and missionary zeal brought him an ever-expanding sphere of influence. They broadened his world while he invested himself in them.

The congregation benefited in immeasurable and often imperceptible ways from its pastor's disciplined life and the personal enrichment he drew from a growing group of like-minded peers. His ministry passions appealed to a new generation of evangelical leaders committed to Reformed theology and expository preaching, and his collegial style meant that Kent Hughes valued and promoted his staff–as he put it, he wanted "to liberate them to follow the fires of their own hearts and fan to flame the gifts God has given them."

The role of women in ministry

Kent Hughes's convictions about women's roles in the church brought into focus the practical meaning of changes that had occurred before his arrival. During the 1970s, College Church modified its form of church government. For many years, a monthly church council conducted much of the congregation's business. The congregation regularly voiced its concerns through elected representatives. Women were prominent on the church council because they served on most committees and were elected by the committees as chairs.

The arrangement gave women and men the opportunity to weigh in at least monthly on any issue. All committee chairs–from the chair of the board of elders to the chair of the flowers committee–had an equal voice and vote on the council, and discussion flowed freely around any matter pertaining to the church. The tradition of male elders was firmly established, but the council model promoted candid discourse on all matters touching congregational life.

The new model elevated the role of elders and abandoned the church council, diminishing women's voices in leadership of church affairs and increasing the decision-making role of the elders. It made administrative sense—the council size kept increasing as ministries grew—but it also made some women feel sidelined, and it situated College Church more clearly among the conservative evangelicals who stood firmly against the claims of modern-day feminism.

The cultural revolution, *Roe v. Wade*, the Equal Rights Amendment, the ordination of women in mainline denominations, and the prevalent rhetoric of "rights" encouraged post–World War II evangelicals to think hard about biblical understandings of gender roles. It was easy to associate the women's movement with support for abortion or the breakdown of traditional families or the broader rejection of authority, and many evangelicals considered all forms of feminism un- or anti-Christian.

Most congregational leaders subscribed to a hermeneutic that limited women's public roles: for example, they believed the Bible taught that women should not be elders, serve Communion, or teach mixed adult Sunday school classes. Others drew different conclusions from the same texts and also recalled women who had been prominent in many areas of congregational life—for example, Edith Torrey (daughter of R. A. Torrey) taught popular Bible classes and led early Christmas morning worship services.

As a member of the Council for Biblical Manhood and Womanhood (CBMW), an association of complementarians that took a conservative stance on gender based on biblical grounds, Kent Hughes identified with people whose reading of the biblical texts circumscribed roles for women in the church. The CBMW's stance contrasted sharply with that of Christians for

Biblical Equality, a group of evangelical men and women devoted to promoting equal access to all forms of Christian ministry. Over the years of Kent Hughes's ministry, the congregation attracted increasing numbers of people who affirmed a traditionalist stance on this volatile issue.

Kent Hughes did not belabor the point: he addressed this subject like others as part of his biblical expositions when the text demanded. But the congregation's leaders tended to agree with him, and church practice conformed to his views on the subject. Women's roles at College Church, though limited, are extensive within those limits. And the limitations are grounded in a particular reading of the New Testament that is tied to deeply rooted assumptions about biblical authority and Christian identity. Even so, women's involvement at many levels is vital to congregational life.

Pastor Josh Moody

Kent Hughes retired at the end of 2006. During his twenty-seven-year pastorate, he presided over unprecedented expansion in ministries, programs, staff, and facilities and led the congregation in clarifying its identity and mission. A pastoral search committee began its work six months before Hughes stepped down. In 2008 the committee recommended Josh Moody, pastor of Trinity Baptist Church in New Haven, Connecticut, a thriving congregation on the eastern edge of the Yale University campus. Moody and his wife, Rochelle, moved their family to Wheaton, and Josh Moody began his tenure as senior pastor of College Church in January 2009.

Continuity and Change

College Church has changed significantly over the years, but it has also remained the same. The most obvious changes pertain to size, programs, staff, facilities, relationship to Wheaton College, and the severing of denominational ties. The church is no longer a neighborhood church, nor does it partner as readily as it once did with the town's other historic congregations. A small community church has become a large church with multiple services, many programs, a large staff, a big budget, and a widely scattered membership. Some of these changes came slowly in response to demographic shifts and cultural changes, while others occurred since 1980 as the congregation embraced the fresh vision Kent Hughes offered.

The constants are readily apparent too. The congregation boasts many of the same characteristics that marked its formative years. It remains committed to the legacy of biblical preaching and social awareness that its early members valued. Evangelism and missions still stand at the core of College Church identity. Christian education holds a prominent place in congregational life. Choirs and robust congregational singing mark worship services now as when the church began. The Statement of Faith has been expanded, but the original Statement still rings true for the membership. The testimonies no longer command the attention that once made them obligatory sermon topics, but their legacy lives on as members are challenged to live out their faith. College ministries remain vital, and members still express their heart for the needy with a "care and share" offering on Communion Sundays.

The list could go on—continuity and change are consistent features of College Church's history. But merely listing the obvious can obscure the challenges that a congregational history highlights. Even a cursory review of the church's past suggests that embracing its legacy requires a willingness to be intentional about certain principles of congregational life, among them: unity and diversity, understandings of church, expectations of the pulpit, and the risks of connectedness.

Unity and Diversity

Arminian and Reformed streams blended in the congregation's early history. Wesleyan Methodists were Arminians, and membership records reveal a curious blend of Methodists, Presbyterians, and Congregationalists moving in and out. It is fair to say that the Reformed inclinations of many early members were hardly Reformed at all in the modern evangelical use of the word. Rather, until the end of World War II, many members of College Church were comfortable with an evangelical message filtered through the Reformed tradition, a tradition that was at once cultural and theological.

The congregation's cultural sense was moderated through New England and pertained to hopes for America and the world, but in the nineteenth century, strict Calvinism was modified by people who helped the nation's Presbyterians and Congregationalists embrace revivals. Even as a Congregationalist church, College Church welcomed people from many denominations and intentionally cultivated an interdenominational ethos. A place where Salvationists, Wesleyans, and Methodists easily mingled was hardly shaped by a strict Calvinism.

In recent years, as the leadership has become more Reformed in the classic sense, the makeup of the congregation has followed. This mirrors a trend within one influential sector of contemporary evangelicalism, and it also reflects the convictions of recent pastors and the elders who called them to the pulpit. It is arguably useful to recall that a bent toward classical Reformed Protestantism was not always much in evidence. Since its beginning, the congregation has consciously chosen to identify the essentials and permit freedom in other areas. The informal church motto, "In essentials unity, in nonessentials liberty, in all things charity," is deeply embedded in the congregation's identity. Keeping it there has always been both a practical challenge and a matter of faithfulness to the past. The congregation benefits from the careful balance it has historically preserved.

The Church

For much of its history, College Church members followed customs rich in theological meaning that linked them to the church universal. Solemn times of preparation for Communion on Saturday afternoons, augmented by questions for self-examination published in the Church Manual, followed centuries of tradition–Catholic and Protestant–of approaching the Communion table with humility and reverence.

Careful screening of members in both their coming and their removal, like active church discipline, kept in focus the goal of being a godly community. An emphasis on baptism echoed the historic meaning of church membership: an unbaptized church member was an anomaly. Baptism was a requisite for the privileges of membership: the church was a community of the baptized. Infant baptism was much more common than adult baptism until well after World War II.

Pastors instructed older children in preparation for their own embrace of the vows their parents had made on their behalf. Adults who professed faith chose baptism by affusion or immersion. The church received members on Communion Sunday morning, baptizing any unbaptized among them, and then people celebrated Communion together as members of Christ's body. Such practices promoted a rich sense of continuity with the Christian past and modeled an understanding of the church as a redeemed community. They also invested baptism and Communion with meaning and solemnity.

The Pulpit

Identification with Wheaton College has always given the College Church pulpit a measure of visibility beyond Wheaton. Financial dependence on East Coast donors made Jonathan and Charles Blanchard familiar figures in the Northeast. Their travels took them to congregations, colleges, seminaries, and denominational meetings, and an awareness of the church went hand in hand with awareness of the college. For itself, the church had faithful pastors and well-connected members, but its stateside focus was primarily local and regional rather than national.

Particular pastors sometimes developed their ministries in ways that gave the church wider visibility: just before World War I, J. G. Brooks, already recognized as a successful statewide evangelist, elevated the church profile especially among Congregationalists, and his effective ministries beyond the church drew attention to the people he served and brought him invitations to wider ministry. In the 1930s, Evan Welsh came to the pastorate with a different set of gifts. An able preacher, he was also a tireless worker who drew students into the life of the congregation and extended the congregation's influence and reputation through the thousands of lives he touched. In the 1980s, Kent Hughes again made College Church something more than it had been before he came. An integrated vision, a clear focus, and consistent Bible exposition over twenty-seven years molded congregational life in unprecedented ways.

Brooks, Welsh, and Hughes, like others who served, made the pulpit an extension of who they were. College Church's wider reputation has often seemed pulpit driven, but the wider influence of the pulpit depended entirely on the person who filled it. Nothing assured that the acclaim accorded one pastor would extend to the next. The pulpit itself propelled no one to prominence. The other principal component of College Church's larger reputation, of course, is its missions giving. J. G. Brooks named a missionary in Turkey his associate pastor and inspired the congregation to provide the missionary's full support. Evan Welsh challenged the congregation to devise budgets that allotted equal amounts to home and overseas ministries. Kent Hughes brought the first missions pastor on staff and instituted programs to encourage the congregation to go as well as to give.

Pastors have enriched the church in imperceptible as well as visible ways through their transparent, disciplined lives marked by generous spirits. History suggests that despite the congregation's size, facilities, wealth, and education, the local and wider influence of the College Church pulpit is a function of the spiritual vision and faithfulness of the person who fills it.

It meant one thing when J. G. Brooks was pastor, another under Evan Welsh, and still another under Kent Hughes. Brooks had little cash, no staff, and no facilities, yet the congregation thrived in new ways; Welsh took on a church hurt by schism, brought it through transition, and set it on its future course; Hughes attracted people hungry for expository preaching and eager for Christian service. Their successes were rooted in who they were as well as in what they did. These and others have left future pastors a large legacy, and they have demonstrated that fruitfulness depends as much on character and priorities as on learning, oratory, or an educated and well-situated congregation.

Connectedness

History suggests that congregational connectedness is another subject worth pondering. Denominational connections extended College Church's early influence by making it a partner in worldwide outreaches. These connections set in place basic assumptions that survive. At the same time, other forms of connectedness emerged. Amid the theological and social challenges of the early twentieth century, College Church members sympathized with fundamentalism and with the conservative Protestant beliefs exemplified by Princeton Seminary professor J. Gresham Machen. These were not the same, and so College Church members differed on specifics while affirming a core of beliefs.

Fundamentalists were premillennialists, and most of them were dispensationalists. Machen was neither, but the inerrancy of Scripture had no abler champion, and no one rivaled Machen's incisive critique of liberal Christianity. Bottom line? Agreement on the inerrancy of the original autographs of Scripture, the Virgin Birth, the substitutionary Atonement, the physical Resurrection, and the authenticity of New Testament miracles. Optional? Eschatology, for one thing. Wheaton College embraced fundamentalism, but College Church maintained a small but important official distance while benefiting from its participation in multiple conservative Protestant networks.

Conservative evangelicalism gave College Church another set of connections beyond its denomination. Camps, conferences, radio broadcasts, revivals, the religious press, and special speakers cultivated a united front that extended far beyond any denomination. Within these networks, yet another set of connections evolved in the 1940s when College Church joined the National Association of Evangelicals. This choice placed the congregation among a group of evangelicals united by specific goals. At the same time, in joining, the congregation opted explicitly to reject the Federal Council of the Churches of Christ and the evolving World Council of Churches.

Denominational connectedness ended in the late 1940s. Robust involvement with the NAE continued for decades, but when the NAE lost momentum in the 1990s, its role as promoter of united evangelical action diminished. College Church belongs to the NAE, but membership means less than it once did. Does connectedness matter anymore? Even the churches planted by College Church have few visible ties to College Church. Further, the congregation's membership mix may make the church seem more connected than it is. Members lead, work for, or sit on the boards of so many evangelical agencies that College Church tends to seem like an evangelical hub. Its networking is not formal, but in recent years, men associated with the renewal of expository preaching here and abroad and authors with ties to the Presbyterian Church in America write many of the books that church members read and participate in the workshops staff attend.

College Church today is closer to modern Reformed evangelicalism than to the Arminian vision of its Wesleyan original members. But the early and unlikely mix set broad parameters that put the congregation on course. Over the years, various kinds of connections, formal and informal, promoted accountability and collegiality. When schism disrupted connections, church leaders looked beyond the congregation to keep themselves answerable and reestablished formal connections as soon as possible. It is still true today that choices about accountability and connection remain important for any independent congregation facing its future.

College Church became a worshiping community before its hometown incorporated, and its founders intended it to outlast the town. They planted a church as a hub for Kingdom efforts, and their successors still work and wait for the dawn of God's reign. Meanwhile, the invitation that Pastor John Welsh placed on every weekly bulletin in the early 1920s aptly captures what College Church historically aspires to be:

> To all who need rest; to all who need comfort; to all
> who need friendship; to all who need hope; to all
> who sin; to whomsoever will, this church opens wide
> its doors, and in the name of Jesus the Lord says,
> "Welcome."

STAYING THE COURSE

A pastoral perspective

by Josh Moody, Senior Pastor

May God the Father, God the Son,
And God the Spirit make us one.
In holiness let us unite,
That we may know the Risen Christ.

KEITH GETTY

CHURCHES COME IN all different shapes and sizes. You only have to read the New Testament to find a remarkable diversity of types of churches with different strengths and various weaknesses. But while there is an astonishing range of relatively superficial elements found in churches across history and around the globe, there is a core of church life that is necessary for a thriving church to continue to go from strength to strength. You could say that Paul's letters to the New Testament churches were an attempt to call the various churches back to this inner core of effectiveness. He was helping them discover a truly authentic way to incarnate this sameness of the gospel in different missionary and cultural challenges and situations.

College Church has had a genuinely blessed history down through the years. Getting to know the congregation and becoming familiar with the people who compose it, I have been fascinated to think through what constitutes the "genius" of College

Church. What is it that has made this church effective for many years? What is it that must not be lost? And by the same token, what is relatively superficial and needs to be adjusted to meet the very rapidly changing times in which we live today? It is this sort of question that appealed to me as I delved into the history of College Church through the expert lens of Professor Edith Blumhofer.

College Church is indeed privileged to have had such a first-rate historian bring her scholarly insight and deep personal devotion to Christ to this history, giving us not a hagiography but a real history and a helpful guide to understanding the church's past. Such work is not easy, and when it is done as well as it is in these pages, it is the wise person who pays attention to the past. Otherwise, in the words of the old saw, we are doomed either to repeat its mistakes or to fail to learn from its successes. This work, coordinated by the much-respected Wendell Hawley and published by Tyndale House with its characteristic skill and high proficiency, will encourage not only College Church, but many other churches too.

Of course, this book is a book about the past. But it is, if read rightly and appropriately applied, about far more than merely the past. Here you will find a catalog of well-known preachers and pastors, stretching all the way back to Jonathan Blanchard, who founded Wheaton College. You will also find stories of less familiar names, but in the annals of heaven they have been no doubt equally influential. But as every historian knows, history is not merely about the past; it is also about what we think we can learn from the past for today—as well as for tomorrow.

College Church's 150 years seems a long time, and it could be a millstone around our necks. ("Look at them! Aren't they old!") But speaking as someone whose college at Cambridge (UK) was founded in 1585—it does not seem *that* old. Really, we're just beginning. As much as one can have a "chronological snobbery" (to use C. S. Lewis's phrase) about the past, where everything that is old is viewed as bad, one can also have an inverse chronological snobbery where everything about the present (or the future) is bound to be worse! Instead, Christians are to be confident about the future, for the future means Christ's return. And we are to be confident about the future of the church, for it is the one institution that we can be sure will last forever. To say that the church has a great future is not empty rhetoric–the church has its origins in divinity and its destiny in eternity.

What lessons can we learn from the past as we look forward to the future? Specifying such matters is fraught with difficulties and is easily liable to personal bias or tribal prejudice or theological axes to grind. No doubt there are many lessons that could be learnt from the history of College Church. Certainly there is a fascinating array of characters that are brought by this excellent book back into the light of day, and there is a deep encouragement to all of us as we realize that our labors are not insignificant. Perhaps one day the Bible study we lead, the floor we clean, the papers we fold, the e-mails we send, will be the stuff of a future book on the three hundredth anniversary of College Church!

Will we measure up to the tireless devotion of those who so believed in the work of the gospel that they gave sacrificially to build a sanctuary even in the midst of the Great Depression? Will future generations say the best years of College Church were in 1890 or 1930 or 1980, or will they say the best years were in 2020? And will those who come after us–we pray they will!–rise to higher levels of godliness and commitment, so that our feeble efforts pale in comparison? Such is the task of "passing the baton" in the relay race of Christian service.

Each of us will have our own list of favorite moments unearthed by this history. I still think mine is the amazing discovery that one of our forebears actually got into a fistfight with another church member! I thought I had seen some disagreements between church members in my time (not at College Church), but even I have never personally seen that. All joking aside, it is helpful to see not just the golden hue that comes from distance and time but also the original "feet of clay" of our predecessors, because it makes us realize that they were human just as we are. They made mistakes, even committed sins, and yet God used them.

Surely one lesson here in this story is the great sovereignty of God. It would be a fantastic mistake if a history like this were to cause us to say (like the Old Testament people of God in their occasional hubris) that God chose us because we were so special. No! He chose us out of his mercy, and this history surely reveals there is nothing more special about the people of College Church than any other group of redeemed sinners, down through the years and throughout history.

While such a history should make us humble, not proud, and while such a history should make us look to the future, and not the past, there is nonetheless in these pages–for those who will look carefully–a message that simply reflects New Testament teaching about the inner core of the nature of the church. It helps us see what it means to "remain in him" that we might "bear much fruit" as he promised, for all our works are really simply Christ's work in us.

As I have thought about this history, it seems to me that there are three particular areas that are worth underlining. And I underline these not so much because I have particular forensic skill at spotting them but because they seem eminently, and fairly obviously, to reflect the teaching of the Bible. I am pointing out some things that you could find in many other churches and that are constant encouragements in the pages of our Bible. But while they are common, they are not commonly found, and therefore they are, as I say, worth underlining.

The first of these noteworthy elements is the ongoing

commitment throughout the church's history to the practical authority of Scripture. Many churches, perhaps all churches, have Bibles somewhere in the building and will give lip service to biblical authority. But it is rare to find Scripture actually taught from the pulpit, and rarer still to find it directing decisions, used in discipleship, and fueling evangelism and Christian education. The Bible has always been the lifeblood of College Church, and that is not only a good thing–it is a crucial thing for the health of any church. Moving beyond worn-out labels like "liberal" and "fundamentalist," the practical authority of Scripture is a key ingredient that any effective church must have. It is the "word of life"; it is the "sword of the Spirit."

The second thing I think is particularly noteworthy in this history is the extraordinary commitment to the work of missions and evangelism. Again, this is the lifeblood of the church; we are an organization that lives by multiplying, not by stultifying. New challenges are coming our way each day in this regard, as more and more people move out of a Christian heritage in this nation, and more and more people immigrate to America and to our community from all around the world. And in this historic commitment to missions and evangelism there is a lesson for the future: evangelize or die.

The church that is not constantly reaching out to its neighbors, that is not constantly seeking to send people to the four corners of the world, that is not constantly and creatively trying to find ways to confront a changing culture with the unchanging claims of Christ–well, that is a church that is on the verge of diminishing. Every church is only a generation from passing away, and that is as true today and tomorrow as it was in the past. But the constant commitment to evangelism and missions is surely a lesson for the future, especially as we grapple with greater missional and missionary and evangelistic challenges (and opportunities, let it be said) than ever before.

Finally, I see that a key lesson for the future of this church and any church is College Church's—what shall I call it?—cultural tendency toward commonsensical unity. College Church, of course, is a conservative church and a church that places a high value on the seriousness of God, reverence for him, giving glory to God, the work of the Reformation, the Puritan heritage of the Mayflower, doctrinal precision, and all the rest. Yet at the same time—and be assured these two do not always go together!—it seems to have avoided, by and large, silly arguments about minor matters.

The mantra "in essentials unity, in nonessentials liberty, in all things charity" has its weaknesses as a rallying cry, because it does not define what exactly is essential and what is not. But the person attracted to that kind of idea tends not to promote a culture of getting hot under the collar about things with which we may disagree. But they also refrain from saying that doctrinal precision doesn't matter. Well, that's a hard balance to achieve, and for some reason or other, College Church (though it has had its moments and, God have mercy, may have again) has avoided more of such moments than many other churches that also take doctrine seriously.

That commitment to the practical teaching and outworking of Scripture, a commitment to evangelism and missions, and an avoidance of squabbles about secondary matters is a combination that—all other things being equal—is likely to lead to a lot of fruit. And so it has proved.

My prayer is that it would continue to do so. As this 150th anniversary year is upon us, we are in the midst of using that focus to help us celebrate the past but also, quite deliberately, to learn lessons from the past in order to build toward the future. Our 2020 Vision, as we have called it, calls us to "The God-centered gospel of Jesus Christ proclaimed in us as a church and through us to the world by the power of the Holy Spirit." We see this vision being worked out in four key values, which we summarize under the acrostic FLOW: **fellowship** or community, **learning** or Bible teaching, **outreach** or missions and evangelism, and corporate **worship** and prayer. These values and driving gospel vision, which are found in Acts 2:42-47, were a key element of the New Testament church. And I pray that as we commit ourselves in a new way to the work of God at College Church, the Lord would be gracious to us and we would see his name honored and glorified before and above all others.

THE PASTORS OF
COLLEGE CHURCH

The Wesleyan Connection in Milton Township

1843–1853	Rufus Lumry
	Milton Smith
	Lyman Beecher Ferris (father of Walter Ferris, 1902-1905)
	Alexander McArthur
	George Clark
	William Kimball
	H. Moulton
	William Whitten
	Reuben F. Markham
1853–1854	John Cross
1854–1855	Charles F. Winship
1855	Joel Grennell
1856	George P. Kimball
1856–1859	Lucius Matlack

The Church of Christ in Wheaton

1860–1862	Jonathan Blanchard
1863–1864	Edwin N. Lewis
1864–1867	Silas F. Millikan
1868–1871	William H. Brewster
1871–1875	James Barr Walker
1875–1878	Lathrop Austin Taylor

THE COLLEGE CHURCH OF CHRIST

1878–1883	Charles A. Blanchard
1883–1889	Albert J. Chittenden
1890–1891	James Brewer
1891–1894	D. Wellesley Wise
1894–1898	William H. Chandler
1898–1899	Charles A. Blanchard, interim
1899–1902	Edwin S. Carr
1902–1905	Walter L. Ferris
1906–1909	William Evans
1910–1917	Jonas G. Brooks
1918–1921	Franklin C. Neitz
1921–1926	John Wallace Welsh (father of Evan Welsh, 1933-1946)
1927–1929	William R. Dodd
1929–1930	Herbert Moule, interim
1930–1932	Arthur D. Penney
1932–1933	Herbert Moule, interim
1933–1946	Evan Welsh
1946–1947	Paul Stough, interim
1947–1950	Robert G. Rayburn
1951–1955	Carl Armerding
1955–1956	Robert Lazear
1957–1958	Carl Armerding, interim

COLLEGE CHURCH IN WHEATON

1958–1972	Livius Poindexter (L. P.) McClenny
1973–1977	Nathan Goff
1979–2006	R. Kent Hughes
2009–present	Josh Moody

FACSIMILE OF THE 1883 MANUAL OF THE COLLEGE CHURCH OF CHRIST

MANUAL

—OF—

he College Church of Christ,

WHEATON, ILL.

⚜CONTAINING⚜

Principles of Church Polity,
Articles of Faith, Covenant,
Testimonies, Rules,
Questions for self examination, etc.

CHICAGO:
COWLES & DUNKLEY, Printers, 112 and 114 Fifth Ave.,
1883.

GENERAL PRINCIPLES OF CHURCH POLITY.

I. The New Testament contains in express precept, or in the practice of the Apostles and Primitive Churches, all the principles of church organization and government.

II. There is but one spiritual order of persons in Christ's Church.

III. Each particular church is vested by Christ, with the right to choose its own officers, receive, discipline, exclude, and restore its own members, and to regulate all its internal affairs.

IV. The acts of all councils and associations touching doctrine and church order are advisory, not authoritative.

V. Associations are a rational means of securing that unity in principle and affection among Christians prayed for by Christ.

VI. Churches should withdraw fellowship from ministers or churches that are unsound in doctrine or disorderly in conduct.

TESTIMONIES.

~~~~~~~~~~~~~~~

1. We rejoice that the fall of slavery in this country has made our testimony on this subject needless. We therefore transfer it to the appendix of our Manual, to stand there for our children, as an honorable memorial of their parents.

2. We hold that making, selling, or using intoxicating drinks as a beverage, is contrary to Christian morals, and if persevered in against remonstrance, should be cause of exclusion from Christian fellowship.

3. Being fully persuaded that Secret Societies are in their nature hostile to the Gospel of Christ, members of such societies who may desire to unite with this church will be required to abandon them.

4. We believe that the habitual use of to-

4

bacco, opium and other narcotics is injurious to both body and soul, and that such use, and the traffic in such narcotics for that purpose, should be discouraged by Christians.

5. We believe that dancing tends to induce both worldliness and frivolily, to alienate the young from the Church, to create distaste for rellgious services, and to place those who dance under influences that are unfavorable to their spiritual well being. We are, therefore, of the opinion that Christians should abstain from and discourage this amusement.

ARTICLES OF FAITH.

ARTICLE I. We believe that the Scripture of the Old and New Testament are given by inspiration of God, and are the only infallible rule of faith and practice. *1 Thess. 2:13; 2 Peter 1:19-21; 2 Tim. 3:16-17.*

ARTICLE II. We believe in one God—the Creator and Ruler of the Universe, existing in a divine and incomprehensible Trinity— the Father, the Son Jesus Christ, and the Holy Ghost—each possessing all divine per-

5

fections. *Jer. 10:10; Mark 12:29; John 1:1-4; Matt. 28:18-19; Acts 5:3-4.*

ARTICLE III. We believe that our first-parents were created holy and upright, that they fell from this condiiion, and that, in consequence, the whole human race is by nature dead in trespasses and sins.

ARTICLE IV. We believe in the incarnation, death and atonement of the Son of God; and that salvation is attained oniy through repentance and faith in his blood.

ARTICLE V. We believe in the necessity of a radical change of heart, and that this is effected through the truth, by the agency of the Holy Ghost.

ARTICLE VI. We believe that the moral law is binding on all mankind as the rule of life, and that obedience to it is the proper evidence of a saving change.

ARTICLE VII. We believe that only those should be admitted to the privileges of the visible church who have experienced a change of heart.

ARTICLE VIII. We believe that the ordi-

6

nance of Baptism and the Lord's Supper, together with the Christian Sabbath, are of
perpetual obligation in the church.

ARTICLE IX. We believe in the resurrection of the dead and a future judgment, from
which the righteous go away into everlasting
life, and the wicked into everlasting punishment.

COVENANT.

You do now, in the presence of the heart-
searching God, profess and avouch Jehovah,
Father, Son, and Holy Ghost to be your
God.

. You receive the Father as your father, the
Lord Jesus Christ as your Savior, and the
Holy Ghost as your sanctifier.

Possessing unfeigned sorrow for your sins,
and renouncing all ungodliness and every
worldly lust, you do give up your all, soul
and body, to be the Lord's, promising, by
the aid of the Holy Spirit, to walk before
Him in holiness and love all the days of your
future life.

You receive the brethren of Christ as your

7

brethren, and his friends as your friends,
promising to watch over them with all fidelity and tenderness; you do also submit yourself to the government of Christ in His
church, and to the administration of it in this
church in particular.

You covenant to walk in communion with
the brethren not only while you continue to
be members of this church, but in all other
places also, in which you may reside, where
the ordinances of the Gospel are maintained,
in righteousness, endeavoring to promote
divine worship and Christian fellowship by
all means of Christ's appointment and in your
power.

And, finally, you agree to live as a humble Christian in the regular and faithful
attendance on the worship and ordinances of
Christ and your engagements to this church,
until by death or otherwise regularly removed. All this you solemnly engage in
humble dependence on the grace of God.

[*The Church will arise.*]

We do now receive you into communion

8

and fellowship with us in Christ, and promise to watch over you with Christian fidelity and tenderness, ever treating you in love as members of the body of Christ, who is head over all things to the church.

This we do, imploring of the Great Shepherd of Israel, our Lord and Redeemer, that both you and we may have wisdom and grace to be faithful in this covenant, and glorify Him with the holiness that becomes His house, forever, Amen.

ORGANIZATION.

I. This church shall be called The College Church of Christ in Wheaton.

II. This body of believers desires to be known only as Christians, without reference to any denomination, yet regarding all who hold and preach the truth contained in our Articles of Faith as equally belonging to the same head, and are thereby free to co-operate and unite with them in carrying on the work of our common Master.

III. The stated officers of this church shall be a Pastor, four Elders, four Deacons,

9

a Clerk, and a Treasurer, all of whom shall be members of this church.

IV. One Elder, one Deacon, the Clerk, and Treasurer, and the Superintendent of the Sunday School shall be elected annually by ballot.

V. The Elders and Deacons shall aid the Pastor in the general supervision of the church, and in his absence provide a supply for the pulpit, and apply relief from the church funds to its needy members. Also, the Deacons shall serve in the celebration of the Lord's Supper.

VI. The annual meeting for the election of officers shall be on the Saturday previous to the second Sabbath in January.

VII. The Clerk shall keep a record of the proceedings of the church, also a register of the church members, with the date of their reception and removal, and a record of baptisms, and shall make an annual report.

VIII. The Treasurer shall keep an account of all funds collected and disbursed

10

by the church, and present a statement of the same at the annual meeting.

IX. The Deacons shall constitute a board to hold in trust all property belonging to the church, and have charge of its financial affairs, subject to order of the church. They shall raise money to meet the current expenses of public worship. No bill or debt shall be incurred without their sanction, unless by a direct vote of the church ; and none paid by the Treasurer without the indorsement of the Board. They shall also control the charitable and benevolent institutions of the church.

X. Persons desiring to unite with the church shall hand their names to some one of the officers of the church, and these names shall be read from the pulpit on the Sabbath day. They shall also be present at the church meeting preceding the celebration of the Lord's Supper, and shall then relate their Christian experience, after which the church shall vote on the question of their reception. If received, they shall, on the

11

following or some subsequent Sabbath, publicly assent to the articles of faith and enter into covenant with the church.

XI. Requests for dismission shall come before the congregation on the Sabbath, and if no objection is made during the ensuing week, the letter shall be granted. In case objection is made, a vote of the church shall be taken.

XII. At all meetings of the church for transacting business any of the foregoing rules may be suspended for the time being by the vote of two-thirds of the members present.

DISCIPLINE.

1. In private offenses the rule of discipline shall be the law of Christ, recorded in Matthew 18:15-17.

2. In public offenses every member of the church knowing thereof is under obligations to endeavor to bring the offender to repentance, and in case of failure to communicate the matter to the Pastor or Elders.

3. In all cases where public fame charges

12

any member of this church with any offense
it shall be the duty of the Elders (others
failing to do it) to investigate the charges
and prepare them for the action of the
chureh.

4. Every accused person shall receive a
written copy of the charges preferred
against him at least one week before the
church meeting in which his case is to be
investigated.

QUESTIONS FOR SELF-EXAMIN-ATION.

These are for use at all times, but ought
to be prayerfully studied previous to the
Communion of the Lord's Supper, that we
may not become "guity of the body and
blood of the Lord."

1. Do I regularly attend the ordinances
of worship on the Sabbath and during the
week ?

2. Do I observe stated seasons of prayer
and read the Scriptures daily, and do I find
communion with God therein ?

3. Do I cherish brotherly love towards all

13

the members of the church, and am I living in charity with all men?

4. Do I aim continually to please God in all the relations and occupations of life, in business, study, politics, social and domestic life and recreation?

5. Do I habitually engage in personal efforts to win souls to Christ? Have I during the past month affectionately and faithfully urged a single soul to come to Jesus?

6. Do I use my property as a steward of God? Do I pay liberally and punctually for the support of the Gospel in my own church, and contribute systematically, according to my ability, for the furtherance of benevolent objects?

7. Do I avoid all persons, places, books, habits and employments which I find to be injurious to spirituality?

8. If I continue to live as I am now living, is it possible that I shall ever hear the Judge say to me, "Well done thou good and faithful servant"?

14

9. (If a parent.) Have I consecrated my children to God in baptism, and am I, by instruction, discipline, and prayer, in the family and with each separately, doing what I can to prepare them for full admission to the visible church on earth and the Church Triumphant in Heaven?

AMENDMENTS.

Any part of this manual may be altered or amended at any time by a two-thirds vote, publice notice being given one month beforehand.

APPENDIX.

TESTIMONY ON SLAVERY PREVIOUS TO ITS ABOLITION IN THE UNITED STATES.

The holding of our fellow men as property is an immorality in practice, and the defense of it is a heresy in doctrine, either of which ought to be regarded as a disqualification for a church fellowship.

15

NAMES OF MEMBERS,

January, 1883.

F. F. Ames.
Mr. J. D. Adams.
Mrs. A. Albert.
Mrs. Selima B. Allen.
Miss B. Arakelian.
Siras Atwood.
A. Austin.
Miss Josie Austin.
E. D. Bailey.
Mrs. E. M. Bailey.
Mrs. Louisa Baker.
W. F. Baker.
Mrs. W. F. Baker.
Chas. A. Bent.
Sam'l A. Bent.
Miss M. C. Bent.
Miss Annie M. Bent.
Rev. J. Blanchard.
Mrs. J. Blanchard.
Pres. C. A. Blanchard.
Mrs. C. A. Blanchard.
C. L. Blanchard.
Mary L. Bliss.
O. W. Bowlus.
Mrs. O. W. Bowlus.
Mrs. Mary Brown.
Miss A. J. Carothers.
H. Chamberlain.
Mrs. M. D. Chamberlain.
Ida M. Chamberlain.
Chas. Chamberlain.
C. E. Chapell.
Mrs. J. Christie.
J. Christie, Jr.
G. A. Conrad.
L. A. Coy.
Mrs. Mabel Coy.
Delia L. Crewe.
Ellen Agnes Cregan.
W. H. Crossman.
Mr. Demarjian
Mrs. Amelia A. Dimmick.
Miss Elsie Dow.
Miss Julia Dunham.
J. J. Dunkleberg.
G. H. Filian.
Miss Tapha Finch.
Prof. H. A. Fischer.

Mrs. G. C. Fischer.
C. M. Fisher.
J. Gleason.
Jacob Grove.
Mrs. Eva M. Grove.
D. J. Grant.
Mrs. Mary M. Grant.
Miss Addie C. Grant.
Miss Alice E. Grant.
Albert S. Grant.
Alfred S. Grant.
G. Gregorian.
Martin Griswold.
Mrs. Martin Griswold.
W. K. Guild.
Mrs. Lydia A. Guild.
W. B. Guild.
Mrs. Eunice H. Guild.
Miss Sarah Guild.
Miss Nellie M. Gurnea.
Dr. A. H. Hiatt.
Mrs. Mary A. Hiatt.
Miss F. H. Hiatt.
Miss Jessie F. Hiatt.
C. W. Hiatt.
Mrs. H. B. Hills.
Rev. H. C. Hinman.
Mrs. H. C. Hinman.
Miss Susie Hinman.
George Hinman.
Herbert Hinman.
Mr. Hulett.
Mrs. Hulett.
C. G. Ives.
Mrs. B. E. Johnson.
Miss Etta Johnson.
Miss Hattie Johnson.
J. A. Johnston.
W. S. Johnston.
F. Jones.
H. L. Kellogg.
Mrs. N. E. Kellogg.
Edmond Kidd.
C. E. Kirkland.
C. E. Knapp.
Miss L. B. Lewis.
Miss Lottie Lewis.
Prof. O. F. Lumry.

16

Mrs. J. W. Fischer.
Prof. W. H. Fischer.
Mrs. V. A. Lumry.
Miss Maria Lumry.
Gershom Martin.
Mrs. S. H. Nutting.
J. D. Nutting.
Albert Nutting.
Wallace Nutting.
Rufus Park
Mrs. May K. Orcutt.
J. A. Parkhurst.
Miss Agnes E. Paxton.
Miss Ella Paxton.
W. I. Phillips.
Mrs. W. I. Phillips.
Mrs. Lefa M. Platt.
Miss Edith B. Pope.
Wm. D. Porter.
Mr. McDonald.
Mrs. McDonald.
Miss F. S. Mills.
Rev. S. Y. Miller.
Mrs. S. Y. Miller.
Prof. R. T. Morgan.
Mrs. R. T. Morgan.
W. H. Morgan.
Mrs. W. H. Morgan.
Miss Maggie Morrison.
Miss May Myrtle.
Miss Mary A. Root.
A. Seamens.
Mrs. B. M. Seamens.
Miss Hattie Sewell.
Miss M. E. Sherwin.

Mrs. C. W. Lumry.
O. H. Lumry.
Geo. E. Sherwin.
Mrs. R. A. Shipman.
H. W. Shugg.
Mrs. H. W. Shugg.
Miss Mary Shugg.
Harry Shugg.
Mrs. F. M. Skeel
Mrs. M. E. F Smith.
Miss A. B. Spear.
Miss Hattie Stearns.
A. A. Stevens.
Rev. J. P. Stoddard.
W. B. Stoddard.
Miss Mary Stoddard.
Miss Maria Stoddard.
Prin. D. A. Straw.
Miss M. E. Strickland.
A. Tashjean.
Miss Cora L. Tatham.
E. B. Thompson.
Mrs. M. E. Thompson.
Fred Thompson.
Mrs. Mary Thomson.
Miss Henrietta Thomson.
Dr. J. B. Walker.
Mrs. J. B. Walker.
W. W. Warner.
O. B. Wilcox.
Miss Emma Wilcox.
J. L. Williams.
E. R. Worrell.
Miss Minnie Worrell.

THE CURRENT
ARTICLES OF FAITH

Article I
We believe that the Scriptures of the Old and New Testaments are given by inspiration of God, are without error in the original writings and are the only infallible rule of faith and practice.

> *"All Scripture is given by inspiration of God, and is profitable for doctrine, for reproof, for correction, for instruction in righteousness: that the man of God may be perfect, thoroughly furnished unto all good works."*
> 2 Tim. 3:16-17; 1 Th. 2:13; 2 Pet. 1:19-21

Article II
We believe in one God–the Creator and Ruler of the universe, existing in a divine and incomprehensible Trinity–the Father; the Son, Jesus Christ; and the Holy Spirit–each possessing divine perfection.

> *"The grace of the Lord Jesus Christ, and the love of God, and the communion of the Holy Ghost, be with you all. Amen."*
> 2 Cor. 13:14; Mt. 28:19; Jn. 14:26; 15:26; 1 Pet. 1:2

Article III
We believe that our first parents were created holy and upright, that they fell from this condition, and that in

consequence the whole human race is in their nature dead in trespasses and sins.

> *". . . by one man sin entered into the world, and death by sin; and so death passed upon all men, for that all have sinned."*
>
> Rom. 5:12; Gen. 1:27-28, 31; Eccl. 7:29; Eph. 2:1-5

Article IV

We believe in the incarnation, death, and bodily resurrection of the Son of God; and that salvation is attained only through repentance and faith in Him.

> *"In the beginning was the Word, and the Word was with God, and the Word was God . . . in him was life, and the life was the light of men . . . and the Word was made flesh, and dwelt among us, (and we beheld his glory . . .)"*
>
> Jn. 1:1-14; 1 Cor. 15:3-4; Acts 4:10-12

Article V

We believe in the necessity of a radical change of heart and that this is effected through the truth by the agency of the Holy Spirit.

> *". . . Except a man be born again, he cannot see the kingdom of God."*
>
> Jn. 3:3; 1 Pet. 1:23; Titus 3:5

Article VI

We believe that the Christian is called with a holy calling to walk not after the flesh, but after the Spirit. Because he has become a new creation in Christ Jesus and is indwelt by the Holy Spirit, yet during his earthly pilgrimage never delivered from the flesh with its fallen nature, he must be in constant subjection to Christ and His commandments by the power of the Holy Spirit.

"Therefore if any man be in Christ, he is a new creature: old things are passed away; behold, all things are become new."

2 Cor. 5:17; Gal. 5:22-23; Jn. 15:10

Article VII

We believe that only those should be admitted to the membership in the visible church who have experienced a change of heart.

"Jesus answered, 'Verily, verily, I say unto thee, except a man be born of water and of the Spirit, he cannot enter into the kingdom of God.'"

Jn. 3:5; 1 Cor. 5:6

Article VIII

We believe the ordinances of Baptism and the Lord's Supper, together with the observance of the Lord's Day, are of perpetual obligation in the church. Recognizing both immersion and affusion as valid, we leave the determination of the mode of adult baptism to the candidate. Provision shall always be made for the baptism or dedication of infants of believers.*

"Go ye therefore, and teach all nations, baptizing them in the name of the Father, and of the Son, and of the Holy Ghost."

Mt. 28:19; 1 Cor. 11:24-26; Ex. 31:16-17, with Mt. 5:17-18

*This article shall be either printed in the church bulletin or read before baptism services at College Church.

Article IX

We believe in the resurrection of the dead and future judgments from which the righteous go away into everlasting life and the wicked into everlasting punishment.

" . . . many of them that sleep in the dust of the earth shall awake, some to everlasting life, and some to shame and everlasting contempt."

Dan. 12:2; Mt. 25:31-46; Rev. 20:11-15; 21:26-27

Article X

We believe in the personal bodily return of Christ in power and great glory as King of Kings and Lord of Lords, and in Christ's ultimate and complete triumph and the establishment of "new heavens and a new earth, wherein dwelleth righteousness."

" . . . this same Jesus, which is taken up from you into heaven, shall so come in the like manner as ye have seen him go into heaven."

Acts 1:11; 2 Pet. 3:10-13; Rev. 19:16; 21:1-7

(This version of the Articles of Faith was amended and approved by the congregation on May 21, 2006.)

A NOTE ON THE SOURCES

THE SOURCES FOR a serious study of College Church are widely scattered. First Presbyterian Church in Wheaton holds the earliest existing church records, since they are also the records of that church's beginnings. The College Church office preserves various kinds of records for the years since–membership rosters, meeting minutes, annual reports, financial records, missionary registers, Sunday school rolls. (Perhaps most valuable for scholars of American religion are two large volumes of handwritten minutes documenting the activities of the Women's Missionary Society before 1910.) Because College Church and Wheaton College enjoyed a special relationship for more than seventy-five years, the Wheaton College Archives and Special Collections also houses primary sources about the congregation. College bulletins, the Wheaton College *Record*, and the personal papers of key church members are invaluable additions to the materials housed at College Church. The papers of Jonathan and Charles Blanchard constitute extensive collections that touch frequently on church matters. *The Christian Cynosure*, Jonathan Blanchard's anti-Masonic mouthpiece, often aired Blanchard's views on local church matters.

Older county and city histories yield additional information about College Church, as do local, Chicago, and national newspapers. Another body of sources pertains to Illinois Congregationalism. The holdings of the Congregational Library in Boston and copies of *The Advance* (the denomination's weekly paper) owned by Chicago Theological Seminary document the activities of the many College Church pastors who held Congregational ordination. Congregational Year Books track membership, attendance, and pastoral changes in every Congregational Church. Illinois Association minutes provide glimpses of the debates and concerns of local Congregationalists. The Day Missions Library at Yale Divinity School holds *The American Home Missionary*, while Cornell University posts digitized copies of *The American Home Missionary* (hard copies are available at the Wheaton College archives) on its "Making of America" site. The Wesleyan Archives & Historical Library of the Wesleyan Church in Indianapolis preserves materials that clarify the earliest vision for the Illinois Institute and its related congregation. The archives of North Central College in Naperville, Illinois, hold information on Pastor Franklin Neitz. Archives of Princeton Seminary and Dartmouth College, as well as Andover Seminary bulletins, offer details about alumni who became Illinois Congregational pastors. Histories of the American Board of Commissioners for Foreign Missions, such as denominational histories and general histories of American Christianity, provide necessary context.

1800's American evangelicalism: p17
revivals, Sunday school, foreign missions,
volunteerism, congregational singing